D1146252

THE   BOOK   OF

STARTERS

THE BOOK OF

STARTERS

LESLEY MACKLEY

Photographed by
SIMON BUTCHER

Published by Salamander Books Limited
LONDON

Published by Salamander Books Limited
129-137 York Way, London N7 9LG, United Kingdom

9 8 7 6 5 4 3 2 1

© Salamander Books Ltd., 1995

ISBN 0-86101-820-6

All correspondence concerning the content of this book
should be addressed to Salamander Books Ltd.

Produced by ZEBU
Editor: Vicky Hanson
Art Director: Vicky Zentner
Photographer: Simon Butcher
Photographer's Assistant: Giles Stokoe
Food Stylist: Jane Charlton
Food Stylist's Assistant: Liz Comben
Stylist: Shannon Beare
Colour separation: Classic Scan Pte. Ltd., Singapore
Printed in Belgium by Proost International Book Production

Notes:
All spoon measurements are level.
1 teaspoon = 5 ml spoon.
1 tablespoon = 15 ml spoon.

CONTENTS

COMPANION VOLUMES OF INTEREST

INTRODUCTION

When planning a dinner party, it's all too easy to devote your time and effort to the main course, yet there are scores of delicious ways to begin a meal, and choosing the right starter will turn any get-together into a special occasion. With *The Book of Starters* to hand you'll never be short of inspiration; it features a tempting and varied range of dishes inspired by cuisines from all over the world. There are over one hundred recipes, including an impressive Fish and Watercress Terrine, crispy Prawn and Feta Purses, a refreshing Chilled Melon Soup and spicy Mexican Turnovers. And if you're looking for original ideas for meals, you'll find the recipes offer so much more than simply tasty appetizers. On their own, many make satisfying lunch dishes or snacks, or you can borrow an idea popular in Greece and Spain and serve your guests a whole selection of tempting small dishes for an unusual light meal that everyone will enjoy.

PLANNING A MENU

In many ways, the first course of a meal is the most important. The starter sets the tone for the whole occasion and should serve to whet the appetite for the courses to follow. It should not overpower the main course, but build up to it as temptingly as possible. Choose your starter with a little care and it will play a large part in the success of your meal.

CHOOSING YOUR STARTER

If organising a dinner party or even just an informal family meal, it is worth taking time to plan the menu carefully, to ensure that there is a good balance of flavours, textures and colours throughout the meal. As the appetite is stimulated by the sight of an attractively presented dish, the appearance of the first course is particularly important. It is essential to arrange the food carefully and to think of ways of garnishing the dish for extra effect. Even something as simple as croûtons in a bowl of soup or chopped fresh herbs scattered over a salad can make all the difference.

Individual dishes look particularly attractive, so whenever possible serve your guests single portions, such as mousses or soufflés made in ramekins

Below, left to right: Parma Ham Baskets; Baked Aubergine Layers; Chicken & Crab Rolls; Spinach Salad; Pears with Stilton Sauce; Prawn & Feta Purses

rather than one large dish, or individual tartlets instead of slices from a single large tart. This also makes serving easier, as the portions can be placed directly on each plate.

When planning your menu it is also important to consider the appearance of the dishes. Avoid serving a meal where all the courses are similar in colour, such as chicken liver pâté followed by a meat casserole and then a chocolate mousse. In the same way, the texture of the dishes should be as varied as possible. Nobody would enjoy a meal where every dish was smothered in sauce any more than if everything was dry and crisp. It is quite simple to add texture to a dish - serve crusty bread with a smooth terrine, for example, or add toasted nuts to a salad.

BALANCED MEALS

Most people today are very health conscious and would not appreciate a meal consisting of several rich and filling dishes. A substantial main course should be preceded by a light and refreshing starter such as a vegetable or salad dish. A richer first course, such as pasta or a cheese dish, should be followed by a light fish, chicken or vegetable dish. Bear in mind that most people are cutting down on their meat consumption, so avoid serving large quantities of meat in both the first and second courses.

TIMING YOUR MEAL

One of the secrets of a successful dinner party is a relaxed host or hostess who has time to spend with their guests. So plan a menu which avoids more than one dish that requires last minute attention. Warm salads, soufflés and accompaniments such as hollandaise sauce are best for occasions where the main course is ready to serve well in advance, and recipes such as tempura, which must be served as soon as it is cooked, are most suitable for informal gatherings where the guests are sitting at the kitchen table ready to eat the food while it is still hot. If you have chosen a main course which requires last minute attention, there are many starters which can be arranged on individual plates and laid on the table well before the start of the meal.

SIMPLE STARTERS

Some of the best starters are also the simplest. These are dishes which rely less on the skill of the cook than on the ability to shop for fresh, high quality ingredients. A simple selection of salami from a good delicatessen accompanied by a few olives and a loaf of fresh bread is all you need for a delicious Mediterranean-style starter. Or serve an attractively arranged platter of smoked fish and shellfish, or a selection of dips with crisp, fresh vegetables. Fresh asparagus served with melted butter is all the more delicious because its season is short,

Above, far left to right: Leek & Lemon Grass Soup; Carpaccio; Seafood Diamonds; Artichokes with Aïoli; Mexican Seviche; Asparagus Tartlets.

and in the summer, when tomatoes are at their sweetest, a simple salad of sliced tomatoes, a few fresh herbs and olive oil cannot be bettered. Avocado vinaigrette requires the minimum of preparation, but as long as it is made with the best olive oil and vinegar or lemon juice, it will be appreciated by everyone. For an extra special touch, slice the avocados and fan them out on individual plates.

VERSATILE DISHES

In some countries, the first course is more of a meal in itself, such as the *tapas* of Spain, the *antipasti* of Italy and the *meze* of Greece. It is fun to borrow this idea and make a variety of different starters to set out in a tempting array so your guests can help themselves to whatever they fancy.

Most recipes for starters can make a light lunch or supper dish. Similarly, there are many main course dishes which, when served in smaller quantities, are perfect for starters. Pasta, traditionally served as a starter in Italy, and fish dishes are particularly suitable for main courses, as are flans and mousses.

Whatever the occasion, simply devote a little time and attention to your menu planning and your starters will always be successful.

MUSHROOM SOUP

25 g (1 oz) dried ceps
2 tablespoons olive oil
15 g (½ oz/1 tablespoon) butter
4 shallots, chopped
2 cloves garlic, crushed
450 g (1 lb) chestnut mushrooms, sliced
850 ml (30 fl oz/3¾ cups) chicken stock
grated rind of 1 lemon
2 tablespoons chopped fresh tarragon
150 ml (5 fl oz/⅔ cup) whipping cream
salt and freshly ground black pepper
tarragon sprigs, to garnish
CROÛTONS:
3 slices white bread, crusts removed
2 tablespoons sunflower oil

Put ceps in a bowl and cover with lukewarm water. Leave to soak for 30 minutes. Heat oil and butter in a large saucepan, add shallots and garlic and cook, stirring occasionally, for 5 minutes, until soft. Add the chestnut mushrooms and cook, stirring occasionally, for 5 minutes. Drain ceps, reserving soaking liquid. Add ceps, stock and lemon rind to pan. Bring to the boil, cover and simmer for 30-40 minutes, until ceps are tender.

Meanwhile, make croûtons. Cut bread into small cubes. Heat oil in a frying pan, add bread and fry, turning, until golden and crisp. Remove with a slotted spoon and drain on kitchen paper. Purée soup in a blender or food processor. Return soup to rinsed-out pan and stir in enough reserved soaking liquid to give desired consistency. Add tarragon, cream and salt and pepper and reheat gently without boiling. Garnish with croûtons and tarragon sprigs and serve.

Serves 6.

─── CHILLED AVOCADO SOUP ───

2 ripe avocados
150 ml (5 fl oz/⅔ cup) Greek yogurt
850 ml (30 fl oz/3¾ cups) chicken stock
grated rind of 1 lime
salt and freshly ground black pepper
2 tablespoons chopped fresh chives

Halve avocados lengthways and remove stones. Using a teaspoon, scoop out avocado flesh, taking care to scrape away dark green flesh closest to skin.

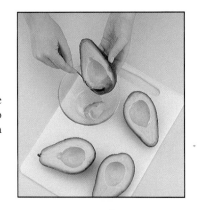

Put avocado in a blender or food processor. Add yogurt and one-third of chicken stock and purée until smooth. Stir in remaining stock, lime rind and salt and pepper.

Pour into a bowl, cover and chill for 2 hours. Stir in chives and serve in chilled bowls.

Serves 6.

SUGAR SNAP PEA SOUP

1 bunch of spring onions
55 g (2 oz/ ¼ cup) butter
450 g (1 lb) sugar snap peas
175 g (6 oz) potatoes, diced
1 litre (35 fl oz/4½ cups) vegetable stock
150 ml (5 fl oz/⅔ cup) single (light) cream
2 tablespoons chopped fresh tarragon
salt and freshly ground black pepper
shredded spring onion, to garnish

Chop spring onions. Heat butter in a large saucepan. Add chopped spring onion and peas and cook, stirring, for 2 minutes, until beginning to soften.

Add potatoes and stock. Bring to the boil, cover and simmer gently for 20 minutes, until vegetables are tender. Purée soup in a blender or food processor. Press through a sieve and return to rinsed-out pan.

Stir cream into soup. Add tarragon, season with salt and pepper and reheat gently without boiling. Garnish with shredded spring onion and serve.

Serves 6.

- BLUE CHEESE & BROCCOLI SOUP -

175 g (6 oz) potatoes
25 g (1 oz/2 tablespoons) butter
1 onion, finely chopped
1 litre (35 fl oz/4 ½ cups) chicken stock
350 g (12 oz) broccoli
salt and freshly ground black pepper
115 g (4 oz) blue cheese such as Roquefort, Danish
  Blue or Gorgonzola
CROÛTONS:
2 thick slices white bread, crusts removed
2 tablespoons sunflower oil
15 g (½ oz/1 tablespoon) butter
1 clove garlic, finely chopped

Peel potatoes and cut into 2.5 cm (1 in) dice.

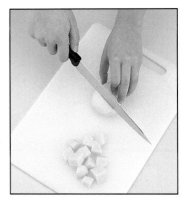

Heat butter in a saucepan. Add onion and cook, stirring occasionally, for 5 minutes, until soft. Add stock and potatoes, bring to the boil, cover and simmer for 10 minutes. Cut broccoli into flowerets and add to pan. Return to the boil, cover and simmer gently for 10 minutes, until vegetables are tender.

Meanwhile, make croûtons. Cut bread into shapes with a pastry cutter. Heat oil, butter and garlic in a frying pan and fry bread shapes on both sides until golden and crisp. Remove with a slotted spoon and drain on kitchen paper. Purée soup in a blender or food processor. Return to rinsed-out pan, add salt and pepper, then crumble in cheese. Reheat gently without boiling, until cheese has melted. Garnish with croûtons and serve.

Serves 6.

GREEN GAZPACHO

1 fennel bulb
1 green pepper (capsicum), chopped
2 sticks celery, sliced
4 spring onions, chopped
½ cucumber, peeled, seeded and diced
1 clove garlic, chopped
55 ml (2 fl oz/¼ cup) olive oil
juice of ½ lemon
salt and freshly ground black pepper
cucumber ribbons, to garnish

Bring a saucepan of water to the boil. Trim fennel, cut lengthways into quarters and slice.

Put fennel into pan of boiling water and cook for 3 minutes. Drain, reserving water. Rinse fennel in cold water and leave to drain. Put green pepper (capsicum), celery, spring onions, cucumber, garlic and fennel into a blender or food processor and process until finely chopped, but retaining a little texture.

Pour into a large bowl, stir in olive oil and lemon juice and season with salt and pepper. Stir in 300 ml (10 fl oz/1¼ cups) fennel cooking water, adding more water if necessary to give desired consistency. Cover and chill for at least 2 hours. Garnish with cucumber ribbons and serve in chilled bowls.

Serves 4-6.

SOUPE AU PISTOU

115 g (4 oz/½ cup) haricot beans, soaked overnight
  and drained
55 ml (2 fl oz/¼ cup) olive oil
2 leeks, white parts only, chopped
1 carrot, diced
2 sticks celery, thinly sliced
115 g (4 oz) shelled broad beans
175 g (6 oz) small green beans, cut into 2.5 cm (1 in)
  lengths
2 courgettes (zucchini), diced
3 tomatoes, peeled and coarsely chopped
salt and freshly ground black pepper
3 tablespoons pesto
Parmesan shavings, to garnish

Put haricot beans in a large saucepan, cover
with cold water and bring to the boil. Boil
rapidly for 10 minutes, cover and simmer for
30 minutes. Drain. Heat oil in a large
saucepan. Add leeks, carrot and celery and
cook, stirring occasionally, for 5 minutes,
until beginning to soften.

Add 1 litre (35 fl oz/4½ cups) hot water and
haricot beans to pan. Bring to the boil, cover
and cook gently for 30-40 minutes, until
beans are tender. Add broad beans, green
beans, courgettes (zucchini) and tomatoes
and cook for 10 minutes, until all vegetables
are tender. Season with salt and pepper and
stir in pesto. Garnish with shavings of
Parmesan cheese and serve.

Serves 6-8.

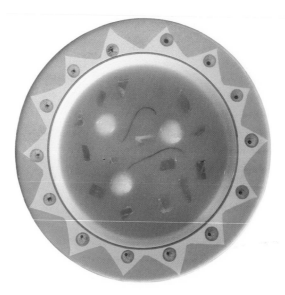

– CHILLED MELON & HAM SOUP –

2 ripe cantaloupe or gallia melons
225 g (8 oz) cucumber
finely pared rind of 1 lime
25 g (1 oz/2 tablespoons) caster sugar
salt and freshly ground black pepper
115 g (4 oz) Parma ham

Halve melons and remove seeds. Scoop out a few small balls of melon with a parisienne scoop, or scoop out 2 tablespoons melon flesh and cut into small dice. Set aside.

Remove remaining melon flesh with a spoon and coarsely chop. Put melon into a saucepan. Peel cucumber, halve lengthways and remove seeds. Coarsely chop flesh and add to saucepan. Add lime rind, sugar and 300 ml (10 fl oz/1¼ cups) water. Heat, stirring, until sugar has dissolved. Bring to the boil, cover and simmer for 10 minutes.

Purée soup in a blender or food processor. Press through a sieve into a bowl. Season with salt and pepper. Leave to cool, cover and chill for at least 2 hours. Trim fat from Parma ham. Finely chop ham and stir into soup with reserved pieces of melon. Serve in chilled bowls.

Serves 6.

─── ROASTED PEPPER SOUP ───

6 large tomatoes
70 ml (2 ½ fl oz/⅓ cup) olive oil, plus extra for
  greasing
1 clove garlic, chopped
salt and freshly ground black pepper
4 red peppers (capsicum), quartered
1 onion, finely chopped
175 g (6 oz) potatoes, cut into 2 cm (¾ in) cubes
shredded basil leaves, to garnish
BASIL PURÉE:
1 small bunch of basil
2 tablespoons olive oil
1 teaspoon lemon juice

Preheat oven to 190C (350F/Gas 5). Oil two
roasting tins. Cut tomatoes in half.

Place tomatoes, cut side up, in one of the
roasting tins. Drizzle with 2 tablespoons olive
oil and scatter with garlic. Season with salt
and pepper. Place peppers (capsicum) in the
other tin. Drizzle with 2 tablespoons olive
oil. Put tomatoes and peppers (capsicum) in
oven and cook tomatoes for 45-60 minutes
until beginning to blacken around edges.
Cook red peppers (capsicum), turning
occasionally, until their skins are charred and
blistered. Put in a plastic bag, seal and leave
until cool enough to handle. Peel peppers
(capsicum) and coarsely chop.

Heat remaining oil in a pan. Add onion and
cook, stirring occasionally, for 5 minutes.
Add potatoes, peppers (capsicum) and 850 ml
(30 fl oz/3¾ cups) water. Cover and simmer
for 20 minutes. Transfer to a blender or food
processor, add tomatoes and purée until
smooth. Press through a sieve, return to
rinsed-out pan and heat through. Season.
Pound basil leaves with a large pinch of salt.
Stir in oil and lemon juice. Add a spoonful of
basil purée to each bowl, garnish and serve.

Serves 6.

──── SPICED LENTIL SOUP ────

2 onions
2 cloves garlic
4 tomatoes
$\frac{1}{2}$ teaspoon turmeric
1 teaspoon ground cumin
6 cardamom pods
$\frac{1}{2}$ cinnamon stick
225 g (8 oz/1 $\frac{1}{4}$ cups) red lentils
400 g (14 oz) can coconut milk
1 tablespoon lemon juice
salt and freshly ground black pepper
cumin seeds, to garnish

Finely chop the onions and garlic cloves. Coarsely chop the tomatoes.

Put onions, garlic, tomatoes, turmeric, cumin, cardamom pods, cinnamon stick, lentils and 850 ml (30 fl oz/3¾ cups) water into a large saucepan. Bring to the boil, cover and simmer gently for 20 minutes, or until lentils are soft.

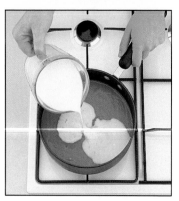

Remove cardamom pods and cinnamon stick then purée lentil mixture in a blender or food processor. Press soup through a sieve and return to rinsed-out pan. Reserve a little coconut milk for garnish and add remainder to pan with lemon juice and salt and pepper. Reheat gently without boiling. Swirl in reserved coconut milk, garnish with cumin seeds and serve.

Serves 6.

— BUTTERNUT SQUASH SOUP —

1 butternut squash
2 green eating apples
25 g (1 oz/2 tablespoons) butter
1 onion, finely chopped
1-2 teaspoons curry powder
550 ml (20 fl oz/2 ½ cups) chicken or vegetable stock
1 teaspoon chopped fresh sage
150 ml (5 fl oz/⅔ cup) apple juice
salt and freshly ground black pepper
curry powder and sage leaves, to garnish
CURRIED HORSERADISH CREAM:
55 ml (2 fl oz/¼ cup) double (thick) cream
2 teaspoons horseradish sauce
½ teaspoon curry powder

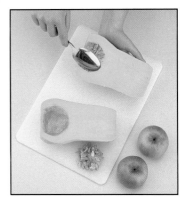

Peel squash, remove seeds and chop flesh.

Peel, core and chop apples. Heat butter in a large saucepan. Add onion and cook, stirring occasionally, for 5 minutes, until soft. Add curry powder and cook, stirring constantly, for 2 minutes. Add stock, squash, apples and sage. Bring to the boil, cover and simmer for 20 minutes, until squash and apples are soft.

Meanwhile, make curried horseradish cream. In a bowl, whip cream until stiff. Stir in horseradish sauce and curry powder. Cover and chill until required. Purée soup in a blender or food processor. Return to rinsed-out pan, add apple juice and salt and pepper and reheat gently without boiling. Top each serving with a spoonful of horseradish cream, sprinkle with curry powder, garnish with sage leaves and serve.

Serves 6.

—LEEK & LEMON GRASS SOUP—

1 onion
2 large leeks
175 g (6 oz) potato
45 g (1½ oz/3 tablespoons) butter
850 ml (30 fl oz/3¾ cups) chicken stock
3 stalks lemon grass
salt and freshly ground black pepper
300 ml (10 fl oz/1¼ cups) milk
crème fraîche and chopped fresh coriander, to
  garnish

Finely chop onion. Trim leeks, wash, and finely slice. Peel potato and cut into 2 cm (¾ in) cubes.

Heat butter in a large saucepan. Add onion and leeks and stir well to coat with butter. Cover pan and cook gently, stirring occasionally, for 10 minutes. Add stock and potatoes. Lightly crush lemon grass and add to pan. Bring to the boil, cover and simmer for 20 minutes, until potatoes are tender. Remove lemon grass and discard. Purée soup in a blender or food processor.

Return soup to rinsed-out pan. Add salt and pepper and stir in milk. Reheat gently without boiling. Top each serving with a spoonful of crème fraîche, garnish with chopped coriander and serve.

Serves 6.

THAI COCONUT SOUP

1 small bunch of coriander
6 spring onions
400 ml (14 fl oz/1 ¾ cups) chicken stock
2.5 cm (1 in) piece fresh root ginger, peeled and
    finely chopped
1 clove garlic, crushed
2 stalks lemon grass, chopped
4 kaffir lime leaves
1 fresh red chilli, cored, seeded and chopped
400 g (14 oz) can coconut milk
juice of 1 lime
1 tablespoon Thai fish sauce
coriander leaves, to garnish

Separate coriander stalks from leaves. Coarsely chop stalks and finely chop leaves.

Chop half spring onions. Put chicken stock into a large saucepan. Add coriander stalks, chopped spring onions, ginger, garlic, lemon grass, lime leaves and chilli. Bring to the boil, cover and simmer gently for 30 minutes. Pass soup through a sieve into a clean pan. Add coconut milk, lime juice and fish sauce.

Diagonally slice remaining spring onions and add to pan. Bring to the boil and simmer gently for 5 minutes. Stir in chopped coriander leaves, garnish with coriander leaves and serve.

Serves 6.

—————— TUSCAN BEAN SOUP ——————

175 g (6 oz/¾ cup) red kidney beans, soaked
    overnight and drained
175 g (6 oz/¾ cup) haricot beans, soaked overnight
    and drained
2 tablespoons olive oil
1 large onion, finely chopped
2 cloves garlic, crushed
4 sticks celery, thinly sliced
400 g (14 oz) can chopped tomatoes
850 ml (30 fl oz/3¾ cups) vegetable or ham stock
salt and freshly ground black pepper
1 tablespoon chopped fresh marjoram
marjoram sprigs, to garnish

Put kidney beans and haricot beans in a large
saucepan and cover with cold water.

Bring to boil and boil rapidly for 10 minutes.
Cover and simmer for 45 minutes, or until
beans are tender. Drain beans, reserving
cooking liquid. Put half the beans and some
of the cooking liquid in a blender or food
processor and purée until smooth.

Heat oil in a large saucepan. Add onion,
garlic and celery and cook gently, stirring
occasionally, for 5 minutes, until soft. Stir in
bean purée, tomatoes, stock and beans. Bring
to the boil, cover and simmer for 30 minutes.
Add enough reserved cooking liquid to give
desired consistency. Season with salt and
pepper. Stir in marjoram, garnish with
marjoram sprigs and serve.

Serves 6.

FENNEL & PEAR SOUP

2 fennel bulbs
25 g (1 oz/2 tablespoons) butter
3 ripe pears
850 ml (30 fl oz/3¾ cups) chicken or vegetable stock
150 ml (5 fl oz/⅔ cup) crème fraîche or thick sour
   cream
salt and freshly ground black pepper
crème fraîche or thick sour cream and fennel leaves,
   to garnish

Trim fennel, cut lengthways into quarters and coarsely chop. Heat butter in a saucepan, add fennel and cook for 5 minutes, stirring occasionally, until beginning to soften.

Peel pears, cut into quarters and remove cores. Coarsely chop pears and add to pan. Stir in stock, bring to the boil, cover and simmer gently for 15 minutes, until fennel and pears are tender.

Purée soup in a blender or food processor. Return to rinsed-out pan and stir in crème fraîche or thick sour cream and salt and pepper. Chill for at least 2 hours. Garnish with a swirl of crème fraîche or thick sour cream and fennel leaves and serve in chilled bowls, or reheat, garnish and serve hot.

Serves 6.

—FRENCH-STYLE FISH SOUP—

2 tablespoons olive oil
2 leeks, sliced
2 sticks celery, sliced
2 onions, chopped
2 cloves garlic, chopped
4 tomatoes, chopped
300 ml (10 fl oz/1 ¼ cups) dry white wine
1 kg (2 lb) mixed fish and shellfish, including white
    fish fillets, mussels, prawns in shells, crab claws
225 g (8 oz) fish bones and heads
bouquet garni
1 teaspoon saffron strands
salt and freshly ground black pepper
½ loaf of French bread
115 g (4 oz/1 cup) grated Gruyère cheese
flat-leaf parsley sprigs, to garnish
ROUILLE:
150 ml (5 fl oz/ ⅔ cup) mayonnaise
2 hard-boiled egg yolks
2 teaspoons harissa or chilli paste

Clean and trim mussels (see page 99). Heat oil
in a large saucepan. Add leeks, celery, onions
and garlic and cook, stirring occasionally, for
10 minutes, until soft. Add the tomatoes, fish
bones and heads, shellfish, bouquet garni
saffron, wine and 1 litre (35 fl oz/4 ½ cups)
water. Bring to the boil, cover and simmer
for 30 minutes.

Preheat oven to 180C (350F/Gas 4). Slice
French bread and put in a roasting tin or on a
baking sheet. Bake in oven for 15-20 minutes
until dried but not browned. Leave to cool.

To make rouille, put mayonnaise in a bowl. Using a fork, mash egg yolks into mayonnaise. Stir in harissa or chilli paste, adding more, if necessary, to give a fiery taste. Cover and chill until required.

Strain shellfish mixture through a colander into a clean saucepan, pressing out as much liquid as possible. Discard contents of colander. Add fish fillets to strained cooking liquid, bring to the boil, reduce heat and simmer for 5 minutes, until fish is cooked through. Strain cooking liquid into a clean saucepan, reserving fish.

Put fish in a blender or food processor with 300 ml (10 fl oz/1¼ cups) of the cooking liquid and process until well blended but still retaining some texture. Stir back into saucepan. Season with salt and pepper and reheat gently. Top toasted French bread slices with a spoonful of rouille and float on top of soup. Sprinkle with grated cheese, garnish with flat-leaf parsley and serve.

Serves 8.

─── HOT & SOUR PRAWN SOUP ───

225 g (8 oz) cooked prawns in shells
2 stalks lemon grass
1.4 litres (50 fl oz/6 ¼ cups) vegetable stock
4 kaffir lime leaves
2 slices fresh root ginger, peeled
55 ml (2 fl oz/¼ cup) Thai fish sauce
55 ml (2 fl oz/¼ cup) lime juice
2 cloves garlic, very finely chopped
2 shallots, very finely chopped
1 fresh red chilli, cored, seeded and cut into thin
    strips
115 g (4 oz) oyster mushrooms, sliced
12 coriander sprigs

Peel prawns. Reserve prawns and put shells
in a large saucepan.

Lightly crush lemon grass and add to pan
with stock, lime leaves and ginger. Bring to
the boil and simmer for 20 minutes. Strain
into a clean saucepan, discarding prawn
shells and herbs.

Add fish sauce, lime juice, garlic, shallots,
chilli and mushrooms to pan. Bring to the
boil and simmer gently for 5 minutes. Add
peeled prawns and cook for 1 minute, to heat
through. Add coriander sprigs and serve.

Serves 6.

──────── SUMMER SALAD ────────

¾ cucumber
350 g (12 oz) strawberries
1 teaspoon pink peppercorns
mint leaves, to garnish
DRESSING:
2 tablespoons balsamic vinegar
55 ml (2 fl oz / ¼ cup) olive oil
salt

To make dressing, mix together vinegar, olive oil and salt in a large bowl. Slice cucumber very thinly, using a mandoline or slicing disc on a food processor.

Put cucumber slices into bowl with dressing and mix gently to coat. Slice strawberries. Arrange a circle of overlapping slices of cucumber on serving plates.

Arrange strawberry slices in a circle inside cucumber, then arrange remaining cucumber slices inside strawberries. Place remaining strawberries in centre. Lightly crush peppercorns and sprinkle over salads. Using scissors, snip mint leaves over salads and serve at once.

Serves 6.

GREEN BEAN SALAD

175 g (6 oz/¾ cup) dried flageolet beans, soaked
  overnight and drained
1 onion, quartered
1 carrot, quartered
bouquet garni
175 g (6 oz) small green beans, halved
175 g (6 oz) shelled broad beans
4 spring onions, chopped
chopped crispy bacon, to garnish
DRESSING:
1 tablespoon lemon juice
70 ml (2½ fl oz/⅓ cup) olive oil
1 teaspoon Dijon mustard
salt and freshly ground black pepper
1 tablespoon chopped fresh parsley
1 tablespoon chopped fresh tarragon

Put flageolet beans in a saucepan with onion,
carrot and bouquet garni. Cover with cold
water and bring to the boil. Boil rapidly for
10 minutes, cover and simmer for 1½ hours,
or until beans are tender. To make dressing,
put all ingredients in a screwtop jar and
shake to mix thoroughly. Set aside.

Remove onion, carrot and bouquet garni
from beans and drain beans. Put beans in a
bowl, pour over dressing and mix gently.
Leave to cool. Cook green beans and broad
beans in boiling water for 5 minutes until
tender. Drain thoroughly and leave to cool.
Add to flageolet beans with spring onions.
Mix well to coat with dressing. Garnish with
crispy bacon and serve.

Serves 6.

SPINACH SALAD

12 cherry tomatoes
salt and freshly ground black pepper
55 ml (2 fl oz/ ¼ cup) olive oil
12 quails' eggs
175 g (6 oz) young spinach leaves, rinsed and dried
4 rashers streaky bacon
1 tablespoon balsamic vinegar

Preheat oven to 200C (400F/Gas 6). Cut the tomatoes in half and arrange in a roasting tin. Season with salt and pepper and drizzle over 2 tablespoons olive oil. Put in oven and bake for 15-20 minutes, basting occasionally, until tender. Set aside.

Bring a saucepan of water to the boil. Gently lower quails' eggs into water and cook for 3 minutes. Drain eggs, place in a bowl of cold water and leave to cool. Arrange spinach leaves on serving plates.

Peel eggs and cut in half. Arrange on spinach leaves. Remove tomatoes from roasting tin and arrange on spinach leaves. Cut bacon into strips. Heat remaining oil in a frying pan, add bacon and cook for 5 minutes, until golden. Remove bacon with a slotted spoon and scatter over salads. Add balsamic vinegar to tomato juices in roasting tin and mix together. Pour over salads and serve.

Serves 6.

──── GRILLED PEPPER SALAD ────

2 each red, green and yellow peppers (capsicum)
3 tablespoons olive oil
50 g (2 oz) can anchovies in olive oil
freshly ground black pepper
2 teaspoons capers
12 pitted black olives, halved
flat-leaf parsley sprigs, to garnish

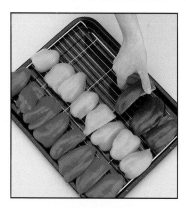

Preheat grill. Cut peppers (capsicum) into quarters and remove cores and seeds. Place peppers (capsicum) on grill rack, skin side up. Put under a hot grill for 5-10 minutes, until skins are charred and blistered.

Put peppers (capsicum) in a plastic bag, seal and leave until cool enough to handle. Peel peppers (capsicum) and cut into thin strips.

Put olive oil into a large bowl. Drain anchovies and add oil from can to olive oil. Season with black pepper. Put peppers (capsicum) into bowl. Cut anchovies lengthways in half. Add anchovies and capers to peppers (capsicum) and mix well. Leave to cool. Scatter with olives, garnish with flat-leaf parsley and serve.

Serves 6.

Note: Anchovies can be quite salty, so extra salt is not needed in this salad.

-ANCHOVY & PARMESAN SALAD-

2 tablespoons olive oil
50 g (2 oz) can anchovies in olive oil
1 clove garlic
pinch of cayenne pepper
4 slices white bread
250 g (9 oz) mixed salad leaves
55 g (2 oz) Parmesan cheese
DRESSING:
1 tablespoon balsamic vinegar
1 teaspoon Dijon mustard
55 ml (2 fl oz/ ¼ cup) olive oil
freshly ground black pepper

Preheat oven to 190C (375F/Gas 5). Brush a baking sheet with half the olive oil.

Drain anchovies, reserving oil. Using a pestle and mortar, or in a blender or food processor, pound together anchovies, garlic, cayenne pepper and remaining olive oil. Remove crusts from bread. Spread one side of each slice of bread with anchovy paste. Cut bread into 1 cm (½ in) cubes and arrange, paste side up, on baking sheet. Bake for 8-10 minutes, until crisp. Leave to cool.

To make dressing, in a large bowl, mix together vinegar, mustard, olive oil, reserved oil from anchovies and pepper. Add salad leaves and toss to coat thoroughly. Arrange salad leaves on serving plates. Scatter anchovy croûtons over salad leaves. Using a vegetable peeler, shave curls of Parmesan cheese over salads and serve.

Serves 6.

—— CRAB & AVOCADO SALAD ——

350 g (12 oz) dressed crab
1 tablespoon lime juice
grated rind of 1 lime
1 tablespoon chopped fresh coriander
salt and freshly ground black pepper
2 ripe avocados
250 g (9 oz) mixed salad leaves
lime slices and coriander leaves, to garnish
LIME DRESSING:
1 tablespoon lime juice
70 ml (2½ fl oz/⅓ cup) olive oil
1 tablespoon chopped fresh coriander
½ teaspoon caster sugar

Mix together crab, lime juice, lime rind, coriander and salt and pepper. Halve avocados lengthways, remove stones and peel. Cut flesh into 1 cm (½ in) cubes.

To make lime dressing, in a large bowl, mix together lime juice, olive oil, coriander, sugar and salt and pepper. Put salad leaves into bowl and toss to coat thoroughly. Arrange salad leaves on serving plates. Put a spoonful of crab mixture in centre of each plate. Arrange diced avocado around crab mixture. Garnish with slices of lime and coriander leaves and serve.

Serves 6.

──── ROAST VEGETABLE SALAD ────

1 large aubergine (eggplant)
4 courgettes (zucchini)
1 yellow and 2 red peppers (capsicum)
2 small fennel bulbs
12 cherry tomatoes
2 cloves garlic, crushed
2 teaspoons pesto
115 ml (4 fl oz/½ cup) olive oil
1 teaspoon coarse sea salt
1 tablespoon lemon juice
freshly ground black pepper
basil sprigs, to garnish

Preheat oven to 200C (400F/Gas 6). Slice aubergine (eggplant) and cut into chunks. Cut courgettes (zucchini) into chunks.

Quarter peppers (capsicum) and remove cores and seeds. Trim fennel, cut lengthways into quarters and slice. Cut a cross in the bottom of each tomato. In a bowl, mix together garlic, pesto and olive oil. Arrange vegetables in a large, heavy roasting tin. Pour over pesto mixture and toss vegetables to coat. Sprinkle with sea salt.

Put in oven and roast for 45 minutes, or until vegetables are browned and tender. Drizzle over lemon juice and season with black pepper. Leave in tin until tepid or cold. Garnish with basil sprigs and serve.

Serves 6.

TROPICAL SALAD

3 pink grapefruit
1 large papaya
3 avocados
3 tablespoons olive oil
2 teaspoons pink peppercorns, lightly crushed
salt

Cut rind from pink grapefruit, removing white pith at the same time. Hold grapefruit over a bowl to catch juice and cut between membranes to remove segments.

Peel papaya, cut in half and scoop out seeds with a teaspoon. Cut flesh into thin slices. Halve avocados lengthways, remove stones and peel. Cut flesh into thin slices.

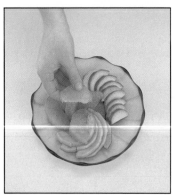

Arrange grapefruit segments, papaya slices and avocado slices on serving plates. Mix together 2 teaspoons reserved grapefruit juice, the olive oil, crushed peppercorns and salt. Drizzle over fruit and serve at once.

Serves 6.

—— CHICKEN & PEAR SALAD ——

85 g (3 oz) rocket
85 g (3 oz) watercress
3 ripe pears
55 g (2 oz/¼ cup) butter
2 tablespoons sunflower oil
350 g (12 oz) cooked smoked chicken breast, cubed
115 g (4 oz/1 cup) walnut pieces
55 g (2 oz) Parmesan cheese
WALNUT DRESSING:
2 teaspoons white wine vinegar
2 tablespoons walnut oil
2 tablespoons sunflower oil
salt and freshly ground black pepper

In a large bowl, whisk together wine vinegar, walnut oil, sunflower oil and salt and pepper.

Put rocket and watercress into bowl with dressing and toss to coat thoroughly. Arrange on serving plates. Peel and quarter pears and remove cores. Cut each pear quarter lengthways in half. Heat half the butter and half the sunflower oil in a frying pan. Add pears and cook, turning occasionally, until just beginning to brown around edges.

Meanwhile, heat remaining butter and oil in another frying pan. Add chicken and cook, stirring, until heated through. Add walnuts and heat through. Arrange pears, chicken and walnuts on top of rocket and watercress. Using a vegetable peeler, shave curls of Parmesan cheese over salads and serve.

Serves 6.

INSALATA TRICOLORE

350 g (12 oz) cherry tomatoes
2 avocados
225 g (8 oz) Mozzarella cheese
6 cup-shaped lettuce leaves
fresh chives, to garnish
DRESSING:
1 tablespoon lemon juice
70 ml (2½ fl oz/⅓ cup) olive oil
1 teaspoon Dijon mustard
salt and freshly ground black pepper

To make dressing, whisk together lemon juice, olive oil, mustard and salt and pepper. Cut cherry tomatoes in half, place in a large bowl and pour over dressing.

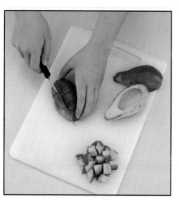

Halve avocados lengthways, remove stones and peel. Cut avocado flesh and Mozzarella cheese into 2 cm (¾ in) cubes. Add to tomatoes. Mix gently to coat with dressing.

Place lettuce 'cups' on serving plates and fill with tomato, avocado and Mozzarella mixture. Garnish with chives and serve.

Serves 6.

DUCK & LENTIL SALAD

225 g (8 oz/1 ¼ cups) Puy lentils
1 onion
1 clove garlic
1 bay leaf
6 spring onions, thinly sliced
2 tablespoons olive oil
2 duck breasts
chopped fresh parsley, to garnish
MUSTARD DRESSING:
2 cloves garlic, crushed
1 tablespoon wholegrain mustard
1 tablespoon balsamic vinegar
70 ml (2 ½ fl oz/⅓ cup) olive oil
salt and freshly ground black pepper

To make mustard dressing, put garlic, mustard, vinegar, olive oil and salt and pepper in a screwtop jar and shake to mix thoroughly. Rinse lentils and put in a saucepan with onion, garlic and bay leaf. Cover with cold water and bring to the boil. Cover and simmer for 15 minutes, or until tender. Remove and discard onion, garlic and bay leaf and drain lentils.

Put lentils in a bowl, add spring onions and pour over dressing. Mix gently. While lentils are cooking, heat oil in a frying pan, add duck and fry for 5 minutes on each side until skin is crisp but duck is still slightly pink in the centre. Thinly slice duck. Transfer lentils to serving plates and arrange duck on top. Garnish with chopped parsley and serve.

Serves 6.

Note: Puy lentils are high-quality, grey-green lentils. Use green or brown lentils if you like.

──SESAME NOODLE SALAD──

200 g (7 oz) fine rice noodles
1 carrot
4 spring onions, sliced
1 tablespoon toasted sesame seeds
coriander sprigs, to garnish
SESAME DRESSING:
5 teaspoons sesame paste
5 teaspoons sesame oil
5 teaspoons soy sauce
2 tablespoons rice vinegar
1 teaspoon sugar
1 teaspoon grated fresh root ginger
salt and freshly ground black pepper

Soak noodles as directed on packet, until soft. Drain and set aside.

Cut carrot into 2.5 cm (1 in) long matchsticks. Blanch in boiling water for 1 minute. Drain, rinse in cold water, drain again and set aside.

To make sesame dressing, in a large bowl, mix together sesame paste, sesame oil, soy sauce, rice vinegar, sugar, ginger and salt and pepper. Add noodles and toss to coat thoroughly. Stir in carrot and spring onion. Sprinkle with sesame seeds, garnish with coriander sprigs and serve at once.

Serves 6.

Variation: Add cooked, peeled prawns or diced ham before serving.

──── BULGAR WHEAT SALAD ────

225 g (8 oz/1 cup) bulgar wheat
1 red pepper (capsicum)
1 bunch of spring onions
2 large tomatoes
85 g (3 oz) fresh parsley
25 g (1 oz) fresh mint
juice of 1 lemon
55 ml (2 fl oz/¼ cup) olive oil
salt and freshly ground black pepper
6 large, cup-shaped radicchio leaves
mint leaves and flat-leaf parsley sprigs, to garnish

Put bulgar wheat into a bowl, cover with warm water and leave to soak for 30 minutes.

Turn bulgar wheat into a colander and leave to drain. Dice red pepper (capsicum) and blanch in boiling water for 1 minute. Drain, rinse in cold water and drain again. Slice spring onions. Put tomatoes in a bowl, cover with boiling water and leave for 1 minute. Transfer to a bowl of cold water and leave for 1 minute. Peel and coarsely chop. Chop parsley and mint.

Put bulgar wheat, red pepper (capsicum), spring onions, tomatoes, parsley and mint into a large bowl. Add lemon juice, olive oil and salt and pepper and mix thoroughly. Let stand for 1 hour. Pile into radicchio 'cups', garnish with mint leaves and flat-leaf parsley sprigs and serve.

Serves 6.

Variation: The salad can also be used to fill hollowed-out tomatoes.

——GREEN & GOLD ROULADE——

450 g (1 lb) carrots, sliced
115 g (4 oz/½ cup) cream cheese
salt and freshly ground black pepper
sunflower oil for greasing
450 g (1 lb) frozen chopped spinach
4 eggs, separated
large pinch of grated nutmeg
flat-leaf parsley sprigs and carrot ribbons, to garnish
HERB SAUCE:
175 ml (6 fl oz/¾ cup) crème fraîche
1 tablespoon chopped fresh parsley
3 tablespoons chopped fresh chives
chopped fresh chives, to garnish

Cook carrots in a saucepan of boiling salted water for 15 minutes, until tender. Drain.

Purée carrots in a blender or food processor. Add cream cheese and salt and pepper and process until well blended. Set aside.

Preheat oven to 200C (400F/Gas 6). Lightly oil a 33 x 23 cm (13 x 9 in) Swiss roll tin and line with baking parchment. Lightly oil baking parchment. Cook spinach according to directions on packet. Drain well, pressing out as much water as possible. Place in a bowl and leave to cool slightly. Stir in egg yolks, nutmeg and salt and pepper.

In a large bowl, whisk egg whites until soft peaks form, then fold into spinach mixture. Gently spread into prepared tin and bake for 15-20 minutes, until firm.

Meanwhile, make herb sauce. Mix together crème fraîche, parsley and chives, cover and chill until required. Gently reheat carrot mixture without boiling. Turn spinach roll onto a sheet of baking parchment, peel off lining paper and spread spinach roll with carrot mixture.

Roll up by gently lifting baking parchment. Garnish herb sauce with chopped chives. Garnish roulade with flat-leaf parsley and carrot ribbons, slice and serve on warmed plates with herb sauce.

Serves 6.

—CARROT & CELERIAC SALADS—

1 large celeriac
150 ml (5 fl oz/²⁄₃ cup) mayonnaise
4 teaspoons Dijon mustard
70 ml (2 ½ fl oz/⅓ cup) olive oil
1 tablespoon tarragon vinegar
1 clove garlic, crushed
salt and freshly ground black pepper
450 g (1 lb) carrots
2 tablespoons chopped fresh parsley
parsley sprigs, to garnish
ANCHOVY TOAST:
6 anchovies
55 g (2 oz/¼ cup) butter
4 slices white bread, crusts removed

Trim and peel celeriac. Coarsely grate.

Immediately mix celeriac with mayonnaise and mustard. In a large bowl, whisk together olive oil, vinegar, garlic and salt and pepper. Finely grate carrot and mix into dressing. Stir in parsley. Arrange celeriac and carrot mixtures on serving plates.

Preheat grill. To make anchovy toast, mash together anchovies and butter. Toast bread on one side. Spread untoasted side with anchovy butter and grill until crisp. Cut toast into fingers. Garnish salads with parsley and serve with anchovy toast.

Serves 6.

— AVOCADO & REDCURRANTS —

3 ripe avocados
redcurrants, to garnish
DRESSING:
175 g (6 oz) redcurrants
2 tablespoons balsamic vinegar
115 ml (4 fl oz / ½ cup) light olive oil or sunflower oil
salt and freshly ground black pepper
½-1 teaspoon sugar

To make dressing, purée redcurrants in a blender or food processor. Press through a nylon sieve to remove seeds.

Return redcurrant purée to blender with vinegar. With motor running, gradually pour in oil. Season with salt and pepper and add sugar to taste.

Halve avocados lengthways. Remove stones and peel. Thinly slice flesh lengthways. Fan out slices on serving plates. Stir dressing and pour around avocados. Garnish with redcurrants and serve immediately.

Serves 6.

Note: Be sure to use a nylon sieve as a metal one may taint the flavour of the redcurrants.

RATATOUILLE TERRINE

10-12 large spinach leaves
salt and freshly ground black pepper
3 yellow peppers (capsicum), quartered
3 red peppers (capsicum), quartered
1 clove garlic, crushed
115 ml (4 fl oz/½ cup) olive oil
2 aubergines (eggplant)
4 courgettes (zucchini)
red and yellow pepper (capsicum) strips and flat-leaf
   parsley sprigs, to garnish
2 tomatoes, peeled, seeded and diced, to serve
TOMATO VINAIGRETTE:
1 large ripe tomato
4 teaspoons balsamic vinegar
115 ml (4 fl oz/½ cup) olive oil

Remove stalks from spinach and rinse leaves thoroughly. Blanch spinach in boiling water for 1 minute. Drain, rinse in cold water and drain again. Spread spinach leaves on a clean tea towel, place another tea towel on top and pat dry. Line a 1 litre (35 fl oz/4½ cup) terrine or loaf tin with cling film. Line terrine with blanched spinach leaves, leaving ends overhanging sides of terrine. Season lightly with salt and pepper.

Preheat grill. Grill and peel peppers (capsicum) (see page 30). Mix together garlic and olive oil. Cut courgettes (zucchini) and aubergines (eggplant) lengthways into 1 cm (½ in) slices. Brush with garlic oil and grill on both sides until soft and beginning to brown.

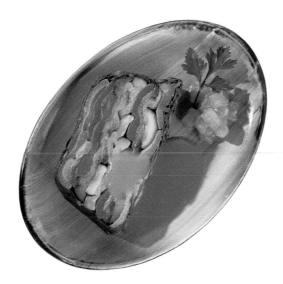

Put a layer of yellow peppers (capsicum) in base of lined terrine, then add a layer of red peppers (capsicum), followed by layers of aubergine (eggplant), courgettes (zucchini), red pepper (capsicum), aubergine (eggplant), courgettes (zucchini), finishing with a layer of yellow pepper (capsicum). Lightly season each layer with salt and pepper.

Fold overhanging spinach over top of terrine. Cover with cling film. Press down with a weight and chill for 8 hours.

To make tomato vinaigrette, put tomato, vinegar, olive oil and salt and pepper in a blender or food processor and process until smooth. Press through a sieve. Turn terrine onto a serving dish and remove cling film. Garnish with pepper (capsicum) strips. Slice terrine with a very sharp knife, garnish with flat-leaf parsley and serve with tomato vinaigrette and diced tomato.

Serves 6-8.

CAPONATA

2 aubergines (eggplant)
salt and freshly ground black pepper
115 ml (4 fl oz / ½ cup) olive oil
1 onion, finely chopped
1 clove garlic, chopped
4 sticks celery, sliced, leaves reserved for garnish
400 g (14 oz) can chopped tomatoes
2 teaspoons sugar
2 tablespoons balsamic vinegar
1 tablespoon pine nuts, lightly toasted
1 tablespoon capers
12 pitted black olives, halved

Cut aubergines (eggplant) into 5 mm (¼ in) thick slices.

Place aubergines (eggplant) in a colander, sprinkle generously with salt and leave for 1 hour. Preheat oven to 150C (300F/Gas 2). Heat 2 tablespoons olive oil in a saucepan, add onion and garlic and cook, stirring occasionally, for 5 minutes, until soft. Add celery and cook, stirring occasionally, for a further 5 minutes. Stir in tomatoes, sugar and vinegar and bring to the boil. Simmer, uncovered, for 15-20 minutes, until thickened. Season with salt and pepper and stir in pine nuts, capers and olives.

Rinse aubergines (eggplant) thoroughly and pat dry with kitchen paper. Arrange in a shallow ovenproof dish. Spoon a little tomato mixture on to each aubergine (eggplant) slice. Drizzle remaining oil over and around aubergines (eggplant). Cover with foil and cook in oven for 45-60 minutes, until aubergines (eggplant) are tender. Leave to cool. Garnish with celery leaves and serve at room temperature.

Serves 6.

ASPARAGUS TARTLETS

450 g (1 lb) trimmed and cooked asparagus
1 egg
1 egg yolk
150 ml (5 fl oz/⅔ cup) single (light) cream
salt and freshly ground black pepper
55 g (2 oz/½ cup) freshly grated Parmesan cheese
basil sprigs, to garnish
PASTRY:
350 g (12 oz/3 cups) plain flour
85 g (3 oz/⅓ cup) butter, diced
85 g (3 oz/⅓ cup) white vegetable fat, diced

To make pastry, sift flour into a bowl. Rub in butter and vegetable fat until mixture resembles fine breadcrumbs.

Stir in about 10-12 teaspoons cold water to bind to a smooth dough. Wrap in cling film and chill for 30 minutes. Preheat oven to 200C (400F/Gas 6). Thinly roll out pastry on a lightly floured surface. Cut circles to fit six 10 cm (4 in) loose-bottomed tartlet tins. Line tins with pastry then press foil into pastry cases. Fill with baking beans and bake for 15 minutes. Remove beans and foil and leave to cool slightly. Reduce oven temperature to 180C (350F/Gas 4).

Cut 7.5 cm (3 in) lengths from tips of asparagus and reserve. Purée asparagus stalks in a blender or food processor. Add egg, egg yolk and cream and blend until smooth. Stir in salt and pepper and Parmesan cheese. Pour mixture into pastry cases and arrange asparagus tips on top. Bake for 20 minutes until set and golden. Garnish with basil sprigs and serve warm with salad leaves.

Serves 6.

──MUSHROOM BRIOCHES──

6 small brioches
70 ml (2½ fl oz/⅓ cup) olive oil
1 clove garlic, crushed
2 shallots, finely chopped
350 g (12 oz) mixed mushrooms, sliced
1 teaspoon Dijon mustard
2 tablespoons dry sherry
1 tablespoon chopped fresh tarragon
150 ml (5 fl oz/⅔ cup) double (thick) cream
salt and freshly ground black pepper
watercress, to garnish

Preheat oven to 200C (400F/Gas 6). Pull tops off brioches and scoop out insides of each brioche to make a hollow case.

Brush insides of brioches with 3 tablespoons of the olive oil. Put on a baking sheet and cook in oven for 10-12 minutes, until crisp. Meanwhile, heat remaining oil in a saucepan, add garlic and shallots and cook, stirring occasionally, for 3 minutes, until soft. Add mushrooms and cook gently, stirring occasionally, for 5 minutes.

Stir in mustard, sherry, tarragon, cream and salt and pepper. Cook for a few minutes until cream reduces and thickens slightly. Fill brioche cases with mushroom mixture, garnish with watercress and serve at once.

Serves 6.

CRISPY WON TONS

1 red pepper (capsicum)
1 carrot
115 g (4 oz) each button mushrooms and bean sprouts
5 spring onions
550 ml (20 fl oz/2 ½ cups) sunflower oil
1 teaspoon grated fresh root ginger
1 teaspoon sugar
1 teaspoon each soy sauce and sesame oil
2 teaspoons sherry
24 won ton skins
DIPPING SAUCE:
6 tablespoons lime juice
2 teaspoons sugar
1 teaspoon Thai fish sauce
1 teaspoon finely chopped spring onion
1 fresh green chilli, cored, seeded and chopped

To make dipping sauce, mix together lime juice, sugar, fish sauce, spring onion and chilli. Stir until sugar has dissolved. Set aside. Cut pepper (capsicum) and carrot into thin matchsticks. Thinly slice mushrooms. Shred spring onions, reserving a few shreds for garnish. Heat 2 tablespoons sunflower oil in a wok and stir-fry pepper (capsicum), carrot, mushrooms, bean sprouts, spring onions and ginger for 1 minute. Add sugar, soy sauce, sesame oil and sherry and cook, stirring, for 2 minutes. Turn into a sieve and leave to drain and cool.

Put 1 teaspoon vegetable mixture in the middle of each won ton skin. Gather up corners and twist together to seal. In a wok or deep-fat fryer, heat oil to 180C (350F) or until a cube of bread browns in 60 seconds. Fry won tons, a few at a time, for 1-2 minutes, until crisp and golden. Remove with a slotted spoon and drain on kitchen paper. Keep warm while frying remaining won tons. Garnish with reserved spring onion shreds and serve with dipping sauce.

Serves 6.

—SPINACH & GARLIC TERRINE—

sunflower oil for greasing
450 g (1 lb) frozen chopped spinach, thawed
3 spring onions, sliced
2 cloves garlic, crushed
85 g (3 oz/¾ cup) grated Cheddar cheese
175 ml (6 fl oz/¾ cup) crème fraîche
3 eggs, beaten
salt and freshly ground black pepper
watercress sprigs, to garnish
TOMATO SALAD:
2 teaspoons white wine vinegar
3 tablespoons olive oil
18 cherry tomatoes, halved

Preheat oven to 180C (350F/Gas 4). Lightly
oil a 1 litre (35fl oz/4½ cup) terrine or loaf tin.

Line base and narrow ends of loaf tin with a
strip of baking parchment. Press as much
water as possible out of spinach and place in
a blender or food processor. Add spring
onions, garlic, Cheddar cheese, crème
fraîche, eggs and salt and pepper. Process
until thoroughly blended. Pour mixture into
prepared tin and cover with oiled foil.

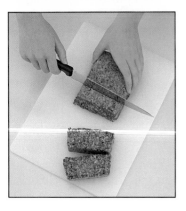

Stand terrine in a roasting tin and add boiling
water to come halfway up sides of terrine.
Cook in the oven for 1 hour, or until a
skewer inserted into the centre comes out
clean. Leave to cool in the roasting tin. Pour
any excess liquid from the terrine then chill
for at least 2 hours. To make tomato salad,
whisk together vinegar, oil and salt and
pepper. Toss tomatoes in dressing. Turn out
terrine and slice. Garnish with watercress and
serve with tomato salad.

Serves 6.

BAGNA CAUDA

2 carrots
1 red pepper (capsicum)
3 baby aubergines (eggplant)
olive oil for brushing
1 fennel bulb
24 cherry tomatoes
loaf of French bread, sliced
fennel leaves, to garnish
ANCHOVY AND GARLIC DIP:
2 cloves garlic
2 x 50 g (2 oz) cans anchovies in olive oil, drained
115 g (4 oz/½ cup) butter
150 ml (5 fl oz/⅔ cup) olive oil

Cut carrots and red pepper (capsicum) into sticks. Preheat grill.

Cut baby aubergines (eggplant) in half, brush with olive oil and grill for 5-7 minutes, until soft. Cut fennel lengthways into quarters. Arrange vegetables on serving plates with French bread slices.

To make dip, using a pestle and mortar, pound garlic and anchovies to a paste. Heat butter and oil in a saucepan. Add anchovy paste and cook for 10 minutes, stirring occasionally. Transfer to a bagna cauda pot or small fondue pot and keep warm. Garnish vegetables with fennel sprigs and serve with warm anchovy and garlic dip.

Serves 6.

Note: Any selection of breads or vegetables can be served with a bagna cauda.

—— VEGETABLE TEMPURA ——

1 kg (2 lb) mixed vegetables, including broccoli,
  carrots, red peppers (capsicum), courgettes
  (zucchini), baby aubergines (eggplant), button
  mushrooms
2 tablespoons plain flour
sunflower oil for deep-frying
DIPPING SAUCE:
2.5 cm (1 in) piece fresh root ginger, peeled and
  grated
70 ml (2 ½ fl oz/ ⅓ cup) dry sherry
55 ml (2 fl oz/ ¼ cup) soy sauce
BATTER:
2 large eggs
115 g (4 oz/1 cup) plain flour

Cut broccoli into small flowerets.

Cut carrots and red peppers (capsicum) into
strips. Slice courgettes (zucchini) and
aubergines (eggplant). To make dipping
sauce, mix together ginger, sherry, soy sauce
and 175 ml (6 fl oz/¾ cup) boiling water. Mix
well then set aside. To make batter, put eggs
into a bowl with 225 ml (8 fl oz/scant cup)
iced water and beat until frothy.

Add flour and beat until just blended. Don't
worry if a few lumps are left. Stand bowl in a
bowl of ice. Toss vegetables in flour. Heat oil
in a wok or deep-fat fryer to 190C (375F) or
until a cube of bread browns in 40 seconds.
Using a fork, dip floured vegetables in batter
and add to the hot oil, in batches. Deep-fry
for 3-5 minutes until crisp and golden.
Remove with a slotted spoon, drain on
kitchen paper and keep warm while frying
remaining batches. Serve with dipping sauce.

Serves 6.

——— PARMESAN ASPARAGUS ———

700 g (1½ lb) asparagus
55 ml (2 fl oz/¼ cup) olive oil
1½ teaspoons coarse sea salt
freshly ground black pepper
2 hard-boiled eggs, chopped
55 g (2 oz) Parmesan cheese

Preheat oven to 180C (350F/Gas 4). Grease an ovenproof dish with a little of the olive oil. Sprinkle with half the salt.

Snap woody ends off asparagus stalks and peel tough skin from bottom 5 cm (2 in) of stalks, if necessary. Arrange asparagus in prepared dish and drizzle over remaining oil. Turn asparagus in oil and sprinkle with remaining salt. Roast for 10-15 minutes, until tender. Transfer to warmed serving plates.

Season with pepper and sprinkle with chopped eggs. Using a vegetable peeler, shave curls of Parmesan over asparagus. Serve immediately with lemon wedges.

Serves 6.

——MEXICAN TURNOVERS——

700 g (1 ½ lb) tomatoes
55 ml (2 fl oz/ ¼ cup) sunflower oil
1 large onion, finely sliced
1 fresh green chilli, cored, seeded and chopped
2 tablespoons tomato purée (paste)
1 vegetable stock cube
200 g (7 oz) can sweetcorn, drained
1 tablespoon chopped fresh coriander
6 wheatflour tortillas
115 g (4 oz/1 cup) grated Cheddar cheese
flat-leaf parsley sprigs, to garnish

Put tomatoes in a bowl, cover with boiling water and leave for 1 minute. Drain and plunge into a bowl of cold water.

Leave for 1 minute then drain. Peel tomatoes, remove seeds and chop the flesh. Heat half the oil in a frying pan. Add onion and cook, stirring occasionally, for 5 minutes, until soft. Add tomatoes, chilli, tomato purée (paste) and stock cube and cook gently for 5 minutes, until chilli is soft but tomato has not completely broken down. Stir in sweetcorn and coriander and heat gently to warm through. Keep warm.

Sprinkle each tortilla with grated cheese, leaving a 1 cm (½ in) border. Spoon some tomato mixture over cheese. Fold tortilla in half to enclose filling. Heat remaining oil in a frying pan. Place two or three tortillas in frying pan and cook for 1-2 minutes on each side, until golden and crisp. Keep warm while cooking remaining tortillas. Garnish with flat-leaf parsley sprigs and serve on a bed of shredded lettuce.

Serves 6.

VEGETABLE CROSTINI

1 courgette (zucchini)
1 small aubergine (eggplant)
1 small red pepper (capsicum)
1 small fennel bulb
2 cloves garlic, crushed
1 teaspoon chopped fresh thyme
55 ml (2 fl oz / ¼ cup) olive oil
salt and freshly ground black pepper
12 slices ciabatta, toasted
300 g (10 oz) Mozzarella cheese
thyme sprigs, to garnish

Cut courgette (zucchini), aubergine (eggplant) and pepper (capsicum) into 1 cm (½ in) dice. Coarsely chop fennel.

Preheat grill. In a bowl, mix together courgette (zucchini), aubergine (eggplant), pepper (capsicum), fennel, garlic, thyme, oil and salt and pepper. Spread vegetables in a grill pan and grill for 12-15 minutes, turning frequently, until tender and beginning to brown at edges.

Slice Mozzarella and arrange on toasted ciabatta. Pile grilled vegetables on top of Mozzarella. Grill for 2-3 minutes, until cheese is beginning to bubble. Garnish with thyme sprigs and serve at once.

Serves 6.

STUFFED MUSHROOMS

sunflower oil for greasing
6 large flat mushrooms
115 g (4 oz) olive ciabatta
6 sun-dried tomatoes in oil
115 g (4 oz) Mozzarella cheese
1 tablespoon chopped fresh tarragon
55 ml (2 fl oz/ ¼ cup) olive oil
salt and freshly ground black pepper
tarragon sprigs, to garnish

Preheat oven to 200C (400F/Gas 6). Lightly oil a baking sheet. Peel mushrooms, remove stalks and reserve.

In a food processor, process bread until it forms fine crumbs. Coarsely chop sun-dried tomatoes. Cut Mozzarella into small dice. Chop mushroom stalks. In a bowl, mix together breadcrumbs, sun-dried tomatoes, Mozzarella, mushroom stalks, tarragon, olive oil and salt and pepper.

Divide mixture between mushroom caps, pressing down firmly. Put mushrooms on baking sheet and bake for 20 minutes, until mushrooms are cooked and stuffing is crisp on top. Garnish with tarragon and serve.

Serves 6.

COURGETTE TIMBALES

sunflower oil for greasing
700 g (1 ½ lb) courgettes (zucchini)
3 eggs, beaten
1 tablespoon chopped fresh basil
115 g (4 oz/½ cup) ricotta cheese
salt and freshly ground black pepper
TOMATO SALSA:
350 g (12 oz) tomatoes, peeled and diced
1 red onion, finely chopped
1 tablespoon chopped fresh basil
1 tablespoon olive oil
1 teaspoon lime juice

To make tomato salsa, mix together tomatoes, onion, basil, olive oil, lime juice and salt and pepper. Chill until required. Oil six 115 ml (4 fl oz/½ cup) ramekins. Trim ends from courgettes (zucchini). Using a vegetable peeler, cut very thin ribbons from two of the courgettes (zucchini). Cut remaining courgettes (zucchini) into slices. Steam ribbons over a saucepan of boiling water for 2 minutes, until soft. Spread on kitchen paper and pat dry. Steam sliced courgettes (zucchini) for 3-5 minutes, until soft. Preheat oven to 200C (400F/Gas 6).

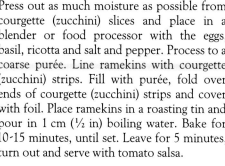

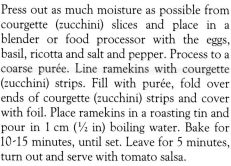

Press out as much moisture as possible from courgette (zucchini) slices and place in a blender or food processor with the eggs, basil, ricotta and salt and pepper. Process to a coarse purée. Line ramekins with courgette (zucchini) strips. Fill with purée, fold over ends of courgette (zucchini) strips and cover with foil. Place ramekins in a roasting tin and pour in 1 cm (½ in) boiling water. Bake for 10-15 minutes, until set. Leave for 5 minutes, turn out and serve with tomato salsa.

Serves 6.

QUICK TOMATO TARTS

sunflower oil for greasing
300 g (10 oz) puff pastry, thawed if frozen
2 tablespoons pesto
10 plum tomatoes
2 tablespoons olive oil
salt and freshly ground black pepper
115 g (4 oz) feta cheese
basil sprigs, to garnish

Preheat oven to 220C (425F/Gas 7). Oil three baking sheets and place in oven to heat. Thinly roll out pastry on a lightly floured surface. Cut out six 15 cm (6 in) circles.

Place pastry circles on baking sheets. Spread 1 teaspoon pesto over each pastry circle, leaving a 2 cm (¾ in) margin all round.

Thinly slice tomatoes and arrange slices, overlapping, on top of pesto. Drizzle olive oil over tomatoes, season with salt and pepper and crumble over feta cheese. Bake in oven for 15 minutes until golden and well risen. Garnish with basil sprigs and serve at once.

Serves 6.

AUBERGINE ROULADES

2 x 250 g (9 oz) aubergines (eggplant)
55 ml (2 fl oz/¼ cup) olive oil
300 g (10 oz/1¼ cups) ricotta cheese
85 g (3 oz/¾ cup) grated Parmesan cheese
25 g (1 oz) pine nuts, toasted
1 tablespoon chopped fresh basil
salt and freshly ground black pepper
basil sprigs, to garnish
TOMATO SAUCE:
1 tablespoon olive oil
1 onion, finely chopped
1 clove garlic, crushed
400 g (14 oz) can chopped tomatoes
150 ml (5 fl oz/⅔ cup) dry white wine

To make tomato sauce, heat olive oil in a saucepan, add onion and garlic and cook gently, stirring occasionally, for 5 minutes, until soft. Add tomatoes, wine and salt and pepper. Bring to the boil and simmer gently for 30 minutes, stirring occasionally, and adding water if mixture becomes too dry. Meanwhile, preheat grill and preheat oven to 190C (375F/Gas 5). Cut aubergines (eggplant) lengthways into 18 thin slices. Brush slices with oil, then grill, turning once, until soft.

Mix together ricotta, Parmesan, pine nuts, basil and salt and pepper. Put a spoonful of filling on one end of each aubergine (eggplant) slice and roll up. Place rolls, seam side down, in an ovenproof dish. Bake in the oven for 10-15 minutes, until heated through. Reheat sauce. Divide sauce between warmed serving plates, arrange roulades on top, garnish with basil sprigs and serve.

Serves 6.

——ARTICHOKES WITH AÏOLI——

6 globe artichokes
1 teaspoon lemon juice
1 slice lemon
1 teaspoon sunflower oil
AÏOLI:
150 ml (5 fl oz/⅔ cup) mayonnaise
2 cloves garlic, crushed
1 teaspoon Dijon mustard

Cut off artichoke stalks and any tough leaves. Trim base so that artichokes will stand upright. Trim about 1 cm (½ in) off leafy top with a sharp knife.

Add lemon juice to a large bowl of cold water and soak artichokes for 20-30 minutes. Put artichokes into a pan of boiling salted water. Add lemon slice and oil and cook for 30-40 minutes, until a base leaf can be pulled off easily. Drain artichokes, turn upside down on a rack and leave to cool.

To make aïoli, mix together mayonnaise, garlic and mustard. Pull out central leaves of artichokes, scrape out fibrous hairs with a teaspoon and discard. Place artichokes on serving plates and serve with aïoli.

Serves 6.

Variation: Artichokes may also be served with a vinaigrette dressing or a herb mayonnaise. Alternatively, serve hot, with melted butter or hollandaise sauce.

─── ASPARAGUS RISOTTO ───

1.1 litres (40 fl oz/5 cups) vegetable stock
450 g (1 lb) thin asparagus
85 g (3 oz/⅓ cup) butter
1 onion, finely chopped
350 g (12 oz/1 ½ cups) risotto rice
pinch of saffron strands
juice of 1 lemon
salt and freshly ground black pepper
flat-leaf parsley and strips of lemon rind, to garnish

In a large saucepan, heat stock until boiling. Keep at simmering point over a low heat. Cut tips off asparagus and set aside.

Snap woody ends off asparagus stalks and peel off any tough skin. Cut stalks into 5 cm (2 in) lengths. In a large heavy saucepan, heat 25 g (1 oz/2 tablespoons) of the butter. Add the onion and cook, stirring occasionally, for 5 minutes, until soft. Add rice and asparagus stalks and cook, stirring, for 2-3 minutes. Add a ladleful of hot stock and cook gently, stirring frequently, until stock is absorbed. Continue to stir in stock in this way, one ladleful at a time.

When rice begins to look creamy, add saffron, lemon juice and salt and pepper. Continue adding stock and stirring until risotto is thick and creamy and rice is tender but not sticky. Meanwhile, put asparagus tips in a steamer and steam for 5 minutes, or until tender. Just before serving, add asparagus tips and remaining butter to risotto and stir gently to combine. Garnish with parsley and lemon rind and serve.

Serves 6.

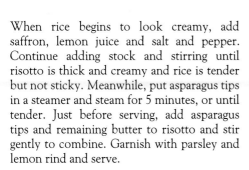

NORI SUSHI

225 g (8 oz/1 cup) short grain rice
1 small carrot
¼ cucumber
1 egg
1 teaspoon sunflower oil
3 nori sheets, 20 cm (8 in) square
spring onion tassels and radish flowers, to garnish
wasabi paste and soy sauce, to serve
DRESSING:
2 tablespoons rice vinegar
1 tablespoon sugar
1 teaspoon salt

Rinse rice in several changes of cold water until water runs clear. Transfer to a colander and leave to drain for 1 hour. Put rice into a saucepan with 300 ml (10 fl oz/1¼ cups) cold water. Cover and bring to the boil. Reduce heat to low and cook very gently, covered, for 20 minutes. Remove from heat and let stand, still covered, for 15 minutes. To make dressing, put rice vinegar, sugar and salt in a bowl and stir until sugar dissolves. Spread rice on a large baking sheet and pour dressing over. Mix gently with a dampened wooden spoon and leave to cool. Do not chill.

Cut carrot into thin matchsticks and blanch in a saucepan of boiling water for 1 minute. Drain, rinse in cold water and drain again. Cut cucumber into matchsticks. In a bowl, beat egg with 2 teaspoons cold water. Heat oil in a small omelette pan. Pour egg into pan and cook over a moderate heat, lifting edge of omelette as egg sets, to allow liquid egg to flow onto pan. When omelette is just set, transfer to a plate and leave to cool. Roll up omelette and cut into 0.5 cm (¼ in) strips.

Toast nori sheets by passing them over a gas flame or grilling very lightly on both sides on the lowest setting. Place a sheet of nori on a bamboo sushi mat or clean tea towel. With a dampened hand, spread one-third of rice over nori sheet, leaving a 1 cm (½ in) margin along side closest to you and opposite side.

Unroll omelette strips. Arrange one-third along centre of rice. Arrange one-third of carrot and cucumber sticks next to omelette, in neat rows, keeping as close to the centre as possible. Using the bamboo mat or tea towel, firmly roll up sushi. Repeat with remaining ingredients to make three rolls.

With a sharp knife, cut each sushi roll into six slices and arrange, cut side up, on serving plates. Garnish with spring onion tassels and radish flowers and serve with wasabi paste and small bowls of soy sauce.

Serves 6.

Note: Wasabi paste is a very hot type of horseradish, traditionally served with Japanese dishes such as sushi and sashimi.

RISOTTO TIMBALES

700 ml (25 fl oz/3 ¼ cups) chicken stock
25 g (1 oz/2 tablespoons) butter
1 tablespoon olive oil
1 onion, finely chopped
1 clove garlic, crushed
225 g (8 oz/1 ¼ cups) risotto rice
150 ml (5 fl oz/⅔ cup) dry white wine
salt and freshly ground black pepper
2 eggs, beaten
55 g (2 oz) Gorgonzola cheese
melted butter for greasing
25 g (1 oz/½ cup) fresh breadcrumbs
RED PEPPER (CAPSICUM) SALAD:
1 red pepper (capsicum), peeled and cut into strips
2 tablespoons olive oil
1 teaspoon wine vinegar

Heat stock until boiling. Keep at simmering point. In a large heavy saucepan, heat butter and olive oil. Add onion and garlic and cook, stirring occasionally, for 5 minutes, until soft. Add rice and cook, stirring, for 2-3 minutes. Add a ladleful of hot stock and cook gently, stirring frequently, until stock is absorbed. Continue to stir in stock in this way, a ladleful at a time. Add wine and cook, stirring, until risotto is thick and creamy and rice is tender. Season with salt and pepper. Cool slightly and stir in eggs. Leave to cool.

Preheat oven to 180C (350F/Gas 4). Grease six 150 ml (5 fl oz/⅔ cup) moulds with melted butter and coat with breadcrumbs. Half fill each mould with risotto. Cut Gorgonzola into six cubes and put in each mould. Cover with risotto, pressing down firmly. Bake for 20 minutes, until crisp. Leave for 5 minutes. Mix together olive oil and vinegar and toss with pepper (capsicum). Turn out risottos and serve with pepper (capsicum) salad.

Serves 6.

— POLENTA WITH MUSHROOMS —

55 g (2 oz/¼ cup) butter
2 shallots, finely chopped
1 clove garlic, crushed
450 g (1 lb) mixed mushrooms, sliced
¼ teaspoon freshly grated nutmeg
2 teaspoons lemon juice
salt and freshly ground black pepper
115 ml (4 fl oz/ ½ cup) crème fraîche
chopped fresh parsley, to garnish
POLENTA:
115 g (4 oz/¾ cup) polenta
1 teaspoon salt
25 g (1 oz/2 tablespoons) butter

To make the polenta, put 500 ml (18 fl oz/ 2¼ cups) water in a large heavy saucepan. Add salt and bring to the boil. Pour in polenta in a fine stream, stirring vigorously in one direction only with a long wooden spoon. Simmer, stirring frequently, for about 15 minutes, or until polenta is very thick and coming away from sides of pan. Remove from heat, stir in butter and season with pepper. Turn out onto a flat plate and spread into a circle 1 cm (½ in) thick. Leave to cool. Cover and chill for at least 1 hour. Cut into six wedges.

Heat butter in a frying pan. Add shallots and garlic and cook for 3 minutes, until soft. Add mushrooms and cook gently for 2-3 minutes. Stir in nutmeg, lemon juice and salt and pepper and cook until liquid has evaporated. Stir in crème fraîche and cook for a few minutes, until it has thickened. Meanwhile, preheat grill. Cook polenta for 3-4 minutes on each side until crisp. Arrange polenta and mushrooms on serving plates, garnish with parsley and serve.

Serves 6.

—SMOKED SALMON RAVIOLI—

115 g (4 oz) smoked salmon, chopped
115 g (4 oz/½ cup) cream cheese
2 teaspoons lemon juice
salt and freshly ground black pepper
flat-leaf parsley and lemon slices, to garnish
PASTA:
225 g (8 oz/2 cups) strong white flour
½ tsp salt
2 eggs, beaten
GREEN PEPPERCORN SAUCE:
15 g (1 oz/2 tablespoons) butter
2 shallots, finely chopped
115 ml (4 fl oz/½ cup) white wine
150 ml (5 fl oz/⅔ cup) single (light) cream
2 teaspoons green peppercorns, lightly crushed

To make pasta, sift flour and salt into a food processor. Add eggs and process to a crumbly consistency. Gather dough together to form a ball, wrap in cling film and set aside for 30 minutes.

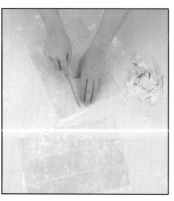

On a floured surface, roll out dough into two thin sheets, 22.5 x 30 cm (9 x 12 in). Cut each sheet into twelve 7.5 cm (3 in) squares.

Put smoked salmon in a bowl with cream cheese and lemon juice. Season with salt and pepper and mix well. Place a small spoonful of salmon mixture on each square of dough.

Fold over dough and press edges together to form triangles. Spread ravioli on a tea towel and leave for a few minutes to dry, turning frequently. To make green peppercorn sauce, heat butter in a saucepan. Add shallots and cook very gently for 10 minutes, until soft.

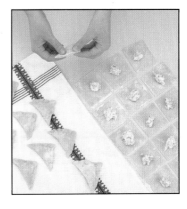

Add wine and boil until reduced by half. Add cream, peppercorns and salt and boil until slightly thickened. Keep warm, stirring from time to time. Bring a large pan of salted water to the boil, add ravioli, a few at a time, and cook for 5-10 minutes, until just tender. Drain. Arrange ravioli on warmed serving plates. Pour over sauce, garnish with flat-leaf parsley and lemon slices and serve.

Serves 6.

ROAST TOMATO PASTA

1 kg (2 lb) ripe tomatoes
2 cloves garlic, finely chopped
2 teaspoons dried thyme
salt and freshly ground black pepper
55 ml (2 fl oz/ ¼ cup) olive oil
3 shallots, chopped
350 g (12 oz) garlic and herb tagliatelle
basil leaves, to garnish

Preheat oven to 160C (325F/Gas 3). Cut tomatoes in half and place, cut side up, on a baking sheet. Sprinkle with garlic, thyme and salt and pepper. Drizzle over half olive oil.

Roast in the oven for 40 minutes, until soft. Heat remaining olive oil in a saucepan. Add shallots and cook, stirring occasionally, for 5 minutes, until soft. Scrape tomato flesh from skins, add to shallots in pan, discarding skins, and set aside.

Cook tagliatelle in a large pan of boiling salted water as directed on packet, until just tender. Reheat tomato sauce. Drain pasta and put in a bowl. Add sauce and toss lightly. Garnish with basil leaves and serve.

Serves 6.

—LINGUINE WITH ANCHOVIES—

70 ml (2½ fl oz/⅓ cup) olive oil
1 clove garlic, crushed
50 g (2 oz) can anchovies in olive oil, drained and
  coarsely chopped
freshly ground black pepper
350 g (12 oz) linguine
55 g (2 oz/1 cup) fresh brown breadcrumbs
1 tablespoon chopped fresh parsley

Cook linguine in a large pan of boiling salted
water as directed on packet, until just tender.
Meanwhile, heat half the olive oil in a small
saucepan. Add the garlic and cook gently,
stirring occasionally, for 2-3 minutes. Add
anchovies and cook gently, stirring, until
they melt into the oil. Season with pepper.

Heat remaining oil in a frying pan, add
breadcrumbs and cook, stirring, until crisp.
Drain pasta and arrange on warmed serving
plates. Pour anchovies and oil on to pasta,
sprinkle over breadcrumbs and parsley and
serve immediately.

Serves 6.

—SPAGHETTI WITH MUSSELS—

350 g (12 oz) spaghetti
2 tablespoons olive oil, plus extra for tossing
3 shallots, finely chopped
1 clove garlic, crushed
115 ml (4 fl oz/ ½ cup) dry white wine
1 kg (2 lb) mussels, trimmed (see page 99)
150 ml (5 fl oz/ ⅔ cup) fish stock
large pinch of saffron strands
55 g (2 oz/ ¼ cup) butter, diced
salt and freshly ground black pepper
2 tablespoons chopped fresh parsley

Cook spaghetti in a large pan of boiling salted water as directed on packet, until just tender. Drain, toss in a little oil and set aside.

Heat olive oil in a large saucepan. Add shallots and garlic and cook gently, stirring occasionally, for 5 minutes, until soft. Add wine and bring to the boil. Add mussels, cover tightly and cook over a high heat for 4-5 minutes, shaking pan occasionally, until mussels open. Remove with a slotted spoon, discarding any that have not opened. Reserve about 18 whole mussels, remove remaining mussels from their shells and keep warm.

Add fish stock and saffron to cooking juices in pan. Bring to the boil and boil rapidly until reduced by one-third. Whisk in butter, a little at a time. Add pasta and toss to coat. Season with salt and pepper and heat gently to warm through. Stir in shelled mussels and parsley. Transfer to warmed serving plates, garnish with whole mussels and serve.

Serves 6.

Note: Take care not to overcook the pasta as it continues to cook in its own heat.

——— STUFFED PASTA SHELLS ———

225 g (8 oz) large conchiglie
450 g (1 lb) spinach
2 x 50 g (2 oz) cans anchovies in olive oil
2 tablespoons olive oil, plus extra for greasing
1 clove garlic, finely chopped
1 fresh red chilli, cored, seeded and finely chopped
2 tablespoons lemon juice
45 g (1½ oz/¾ cup) fresh breadcrumbs
25 g (1 oz/¼ cup) grated Parmesan cheese
strips of lemon rind, to garnish

Cook pasta in a large pan of boiling salted water as directed on packet, until just tender.

Meanwhile, wash spinach and put in a large saucepan with only the water that clings to the leaves. Cook for 2-3 minutes, until wilted. Drain thoroughly, coarsely chop and set aside. Put anchovies and their oil in a saucepan with olive oil, garlic and chilli. Cook over gentle heat, stirring occasionally, for 5 minutes, or until anchovies break down to a smooth consistency. Stir in lemon juice, half the breadcrumbs and spinach. Preheat oven to 200C (400F/Gas 6).

Drain pasta, rinse in cold water and drain again. Divide spinach mixture among shells. Brush an ovenproof dish with oil and arrange stuffed shells in dish. Sprinkle with remaining breadcrumbs and Parmesan and bake in the oven for 8 minutes. Garnish with lemon rind and serve immediately.

Serves 6.

—PENNE WITH SWEET PEPPERS—

3 red peppers (capsicum)
3 yellow peppers (capsicum)
55 ml (2 fl oz / ¼ cup) olive oil
2 shallots, finely chopped
1 clove garlic, finely chopped
salt and freshly ground black pepper
350 g (12 oz) penne
2 teaspoons capers, chopped
1 teaspoon chopped fresh parsley
1 teaspoon chopped fresh tarragon

Preheat grill. Cut peppers (capsicum) into quarters and remove cores and seeds. Place, skin side up, under a hot grill and grill until skin is charred and blistered.

Put peppers (capsicum) in a plastic bag, seal and leave until cool enough to handle. Peel, then cut into strips about the same size as the pasta. Heat oil in a saucepan, add shallots, garlic and peppers (capsicum), cover and cook, stirring occasionally, for 10 minutes. Remove lid and cook over a high heat, stirring frequently, for 5 minutes. Season with salt and pepper.

Meanwhile, cook pasta in a large pan of boiling salted water as directed on packet, until just tender. Drain and return to saucepan. Stir in pepper (capsicum) mixture, capers, parsley and tarragon and serve.

Serves 6.

— RIGATONI WITH ASPARAGUS —

450 g (1 lb) asparagus
115 ml (4 fl oz/½ cup) crème fraîche
salt and freshly ground black pepper
2 tablespoons chopped fresh chives
350 g (12 oz) rigatoni
chives, to garnish

Snap woody ends from asparagus stalks and peel off any tough skin. Cut off tips. Cut stalks into 2.5 cm (1 in) pieces.

Add asparagus stalks to a saucepan of boiling salted water, put tips in a steamer and place above water. Simmer for 10 minutes, until stalks are very tender. Remove tips and keep warm. Drain stalks, reserving cooking liquid. Put stalks in a blender or food processor with 150 ml (5 fl oz/⅔ cup) cooking liquid and crème fraîche. Process until smooth.

Return to pan and reheat gently. Season with salt and pepper and stir in chives. Meanwhile, cook pasta in a large pan of boiling salted water as directed on packet, until just tender. Drain and arrange on warmed serving plates. Pour over sauce, garnish with asparagus tips and chives and serve immediately.

Serves 6.

—CHEESE & TOMATO FUSILLI—

350 g (12 oz) fusilli
55 ml (2 fl oz/ ¼ cup) olive oil
1 bunch of spring onions, chopped
1 clove garlic
salt and freshly ground black pepper
225 g (8 oz) cherry tomatoes, quartered
150 g (5 oz) Mozzarella cheese, diced
55 g (2 oz/ ½ cup) grated Parmesan cheese
1 small bunch of basil
12 pitted black olives, halved

Cook pasta in a large pan of boiling salted water as directed on packet, until just tender.

Meanwhile, heat olive oil in a small saucepan. Add spring onions and cook, stirring occasionally, for 2-3 minutes. Add garlic and cook for 2 minutes. Drain pasta and return to saucepan. Add spring onion mixture and salt and pepper.

Add tomatoes to pasta and stir over a gentle heat, to warm through. Stir in Mozzarella and Parmesan. Coarsely tear basil leaves, add to pasta with olives and serve immediately.

Serves 6.

SPINACH TAGLIATELLE

300 g (10 oz) spinach
2 tablespoons olive oil
1 clove garlic
150 ml (5 fl oz/²⁄₃ cup) double (thick) cream
115 g (4 oz) Mascarpone cheese
salt and freshly ground black pepper
350 g (12 oz) tagliatelle

Wash and dry spinach and chop very finely.
Heat oil in a large saucepan. Add garlic clove
and cook until browned. Remove with a
slotted spoon and discard. Add spinach to
pan and cook, stirring, for 2-3 minutes, until
wilted and tender.

Put cream, Mascarpone and salt and pepper
in a saucepan and bring to the boil, stirring.
Simmer for a few minutes, until thickened.
Meanwhile, cook tagliatelle in a large pan of
boiling salted water as directed on packet,
until just tender.

Drain pasta, reserving cooking water, and
return to saucepan. Add enough of cooking
liquid to cream sauce to give a smooth
pouring consistency. Pour onto pasta. Add
spinach and toss to coat. Serve immediately.

Serves 6.

——GOATS' CHEESE SOUFFLÉS——

225 ml (8 fl oz/scant cup) milk
1 shallot, finely chopped
1 bay leaf
6 black peppercorns
3 tablespoons butter, plus extra for greasing
45 g (1½ oz/⅓ cup) plain flour
115 g (4 oz) goats' cheese
3 eggs, size 2, separated
1 tablespoon chopped fresh chives
salt and freshly ground black pepper
150 ml (5 fl oz/⅔ cup) double (thick) cream
25 g (1 oz/¼ cup) coarsely grated Parmesan cheese
lamb's lettuce and hazelnuts, to garnish

Preheat oven to 180C (350F/Gas 4). Butter six 150 ml (5 fl oz/⅔ cup) ramekins. Put milk, shallot, bay leaf and peppercorns in a saucepan and bring slowly to the boil. Strain into a jug. Melt butter in a saucepan, add flour and cook, stirring, for 1-2 minutes. Remove from heat and gradually stir in milk. Simmer gently for 2-3 minutes. Crumble in goats' cheese and stir until melted. Stir in egg yolks, chives and salt and pepper. Remove from heat. Whisk egg whites until holding soft peaks and fold into cheese mixture.

Spoon into prepared ramekins. Stand dishes in a roasting tin and pour boiling water into tin to come one-third up the sides of ramekins. Bake for 15-20 minutes, until firm. Leave to cool. When ready to serve, preheat oven to 200C (400F/Gas 6). Run a knife round sides of ramekins and turn soufflés into a shallow ovenproof dish. Pour over cream, sprinkle with Parmesan and bake for 10-15 minutes, until golden. Garnish with lamb's lettuce and hazelnuts and serve.

Serves 6.

ANCHOVY EGGS

butter for greasing
50 g (2 oz) can anchovies in olive oil
6 eggs
salt and freshly ground black pepper
150 ml (5 fl oz/⅔ cup) double (thick) cream
2 tablespoons chopped fresh tarragon
25 g (1 oz/½ cup) fresh breadcrumbs
tarragon sprigs, to garnish

Preheat oven to 180C (350F/Gas 4). Butter six ramekins. Drain anchovies, reserving oil, and coarsely chop. Divide anchovies among ramekins. Carefully break an egg into each and season with salt and pepper.

Place ramekins in a roasting tin. Pour boiling water into tin to come halfway up sides of ramekins. Bake in the oven for 6 minutes, or until eggs are just set. Spoon cream over eggs and sprinkle with chopped tarragon. Return to the oven for 2-3 minutes.

Meanwhile, heat anchovy oil in a frying pan. Add breadcrumbs and cook, stirring, until crisp and golden. Place each ramekin on a serving plate and sprinkle with breadcrumbs. Garnish with tarragon sprigs and serve.

Serves 6.

——— FETA & HERB POPOVERS ———

1 tablespoon sunflower oil
225 ml (8 fl oz/scant cup) milk
15 g (½ oz/1 tablespoon) melted butter
2 eggs, beaten
85 g (3 oz/¾ cup) plain flour
2 teaspoons chopped fresh chives
2 teaspoons chopped fresh parsley
salt and freshly ground black pepper
115 g (4 oz) feta cheese, cut into 24 cubes
flat-leaf parsley and chopped fresh chives, to garnish
MANGO SAUCE:
2 tablespoons mango chutney
175 ml (6 fl oz/¾ cup) Greek yogurt

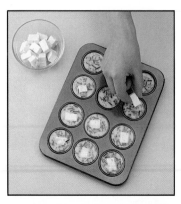

Preheat oven to 220C (425F/Gas 7). Brush the cups in two mini muffin tins with oil and put in the oven to heat. Stir milk and melted butter into eggs. Sift flour into egg mixture and whisk together to make a smooth batter. Stir in chives, parsley and salt and pepper. Fill each muffin cup with batter. Put a cube of feta cheese in the centre of each one and bake in the oven for 20-25 minutes, until risen and golden.

Meanwhile, make mango sauce. Put mango chutney in a bowl, chopping any large pieces of fruit. Stir in yogurt. Arrange popovers on serving plates. Garnish with flat-leaf parsley and chives and serve with mango sauce.

Serves 4-6.

— PEARS WITH STILTON SAUCE —

3 large pears
1 tablespoon lemon juice
chervil leaves, to garnish
STILTON SAUCE:
115 ml (4 fl oz/½ cup) crème fraîche
2 tablespoons milk
85 g (3 oz) Stilton cheese
1-2 teaspoons lemon juice
2 teaspoons poppy seeds
salt and freshly ground black pepper

To make the Stilton sauce, put crème fraîche and milk in a saucepan and heat gently. Crumble in Stilton and stir until melted.

Remove pan from heat, stir in lemon juice, poppy seeds and salt and pepper and leave to cool. Cut each pear lengthways in half, keeping stalk intact if possible. Using a small sharp knife, cut out core. Brush lemon juice over cut surfaces.

Divide Stilton sauce among six serving plates. Slice each pear half lengthways and arrange on top of sauce, in a fan shape. Garnish with chervil leaves and serve.

Serves 6.

—QUAILS' EGGS IN FILO NESTS—

12 quails' eggs
25 g (1 oz/2 tablespoons) butter, melted
3 sheets filo pastry, 40 x 30 cm (16 x 12 in)
tarragon leaves, to garnish
MUSHROOM DUXELLE:
350 g (12 oz) button mushrooms
25 g (1 oz/2 tablespoons) butter
2 shallots, finely chopped
pinch of freshly grated nutmeg
salt and freshly ground black pepper
CREAM SAUCE:
2 egg yolks
4 teaspoons lemon juice
115 g (4 oz/½ cup) butter
70 ml (2½ fl oz/⅓ cup) double (thick) cream
1 tablespoon chopped fresh tarragon

Preheat oven to 190C (375F/Gas 5). To make mushroom duxelle, finely chop mushrooms in a food processor or by hand. Heat butter in a saucepan. Add shallots and cook, stirring occasionally, for 5 minutes, until soft. Add chopped mushrooms and cook gently, stirring occasionally, for 5 minutes, until soft. Increase the heat and cook until any liquid has evaporated. Season with nutmeg and salt and pepper and set aside.

Bring a saucepan of water to the boil. Lower quails' eggs into water and boil for 1 minute. Put eggs in a colander and rinse with cold water. Carefully peel eggs. Heat some water in a saucepan, but do not boil. Put peeled eggs in the water to keep warm.

To make filo nests, turn six 7.5 cm (3 in) ramekins upside down and lightly brush all over with melted butter. Cut the pastry into eighteen 12.5 cm (5 in) squares. Brush a square with butter and press, butter side up, over an upturned ramekin. Butter a second square of filo and press over the first piece, arranging it at an angle so that the points form petals. Repeat with a third piece. Cover remaining ramekins in the same way. Bake for 10-15 minutes, until crisp and golden. Carefully lift off pastry nests and place, right side up, on a baking sheet. Keep warm.

To make cream sauce, put egg yolks in a bowl set over a pan of simmering water. Whisk in lemon juice and heat gently until warm. Put butter in a small saucepan and heat very gently until melted. Gradually whisk in egg yolk mixture until mixture thickens. Stir in cream, tarragon and salt and pepper. Reheat mushroom duxelle.

Put a filo nest on each of six warmed serving plates. Divide mushroom duxelle between nests. Arrange two quails' eggs in each nest. Spoon over cream sauce, garnish with tarragon leaves and serve at once.

Serves 6.

Note: Filo pastry is available in different sizes, so you may have to adjust the number of sheets needed, depending on their size.

——GORGONZOLA TARTLETS——

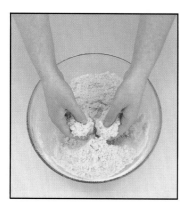

6 spring onions, chopped
115 g (4 oz) Gorgonzola cheese, crumbled
2 eggs, beaten
250 ml (9 fl oz/1 cup) whipping cream
salt and freshly ground black pepper
SHORTCRUST PASTRY:
300 g (10 oz/2 ½ cups) plain flour
150 g (5 oz/⅔ cup) butter, diced

To make shortcrust pastry, sift flour into a bowl. Rub in butter until mixture resembles fine breadcrumbs.

Stir in about 8 teaspoons cold water to bind to a smooth dough. Wrap in cling film and chill for 30 minutes. Preheat oven to 200C (400F/Gas 6). Thinly roll out pastry on a lightly floured surface. Cut circles to fit six 10 cm (4 in) loose-bottomed tartlet tins. Line tins with pastry then press foil or greaseproof paper into pastry cases. Fill with baking beans and bake for 15 minutes. Reduce oven temperature to 190C (375F/Gas 5).

Remove beans and foil, carefully remove pastry cases from tins and transfer to a baking sheet. Arrange spring onions and cheese in pastry cases. Mix together eggs, cream and salt and pepper and pour into pastry cases. Bake for 15 minutes, until set and golden. Serve warm.

Serves 6.

SPINACH GNOCCHI

450 g (1 lb) frozen leaf spinach
225 g (8 oz/1 cup) ricotta cheese
115 g (4 oz/1 cup) plain flour
2 eggs, beaten
pinch of freshly grated nutmeg
salt and freshly ground black pepper
24 cherry tomatoes
sunflower oil for greasing
85 g (3 oz/⅓ cup) butter
55 g (2 oz) Parmesan cheese

Cook spinach as directed on packet. Drain well and squeeze dry. Chop very finely in a food processor and leave to cool.

In a bowl, mix together spinach, ricotta, flour, eggs, nutmeg and salt and pepper. With floured hands, form mixture into small sausage shapes, about 2 cm (¾ in) long. Chill for at least 1 hour, until firm. Meanwhile, preheat oven to 200C (400F/Gas 6). Oil a roasting tin. Cut tomatoes in half and arrange, cut side up, in tin. Season with salt and pepper and roast for 20 minutes.

Bring a large pan of salted water to the boil. Drop spinach gnocchi, a few at a time, into water. As they rise to the surface and float, remove with a slotted spoon. Drain thoroughly and keep warm while cooking remaining gnocchi. Heat butter in a saucepan. Add gnocchi and roasted tomatoes and stir gently to coat with butter. Divide among six warmed serving plates. Using a vegetable peeler, shave curls of Parmesan over gnocchi and serve.

Serves 6.

— FRUITY ROQUEFORT PARCELS —

1 ripe mango
115 g (4 oz) Roquefort cheese
1 teaspoon lime juice
freshly ground black pepper
8 sheets filo pastry, 20 x 30 cm (8 x 12 in)
55 g (2 oz/¼ cup) butter, melted
strips of lime rind and mint leaves, to garnish
CUCUMBER SALSA:
½ cucumber, peeled, seeded and diced
grated rind of 1 lime
1 teaspoon lime juice
1 teaspoon chopped fresh mint

Peel mango, cut flesh away from stone and cut flesh into small dice.

Cut Roquefort cheese into small dice. Mix together mango, cheese, lime juice and pepper. Lightly brush a sheet of filo pastry with melted butter. Layer three more sheets on top, brushing each one with butter. Layer remaining four sheets in the same way. Cut each piece of pastry into three 10 cm (4 in) wide strips. Brush a baking sheet with butter. Preheat oven to 220C (425F/Gas 7).

Place a spoonful of mango filling in one corner of a strip and diagonally fold over the corner. Continue folding over the filled corner of pastry to form a triangular parcel. Place on baking sheet and brush lightly with butter. Repeat with remaining pastry and filling. Bake for 7-10 minutes, until golden brown. To make cucumber salsa, mix together cucumber, lime rind and juice and mint. Garnish triangles with lime rind and mint leaves and serve with cucumber salsa.

Serves 6.

DEEP-FRIED BRIE

175 g (6 oz) firm Brie, chilled
2 eggs
salt and freshly ground black pepper
75 g (3 oz/1 ½ cups) fresh breadcrumbs
sunflower oil for deep-frying
strips of orange rind, to garnish
CRANBERRY RELISH:
2 tablespoons sunflower oil
1 onion, finely chopped
1 eating apple, peeled, cored and chopped
175 g (6 oz) cranberries
grated rind and juice of 1 orange
1 cinnamon stick
85 g (3 oz/⅓ cup) soft brown sugar

Cut cheese into six wedges and trim off rind.

To make cranberry relish, heat oil in a saucepan, add onion and cook, stirring occasionally, for 5 minutes, until soft. Add apple, cranberries, orange rind and juice, cinnamon stick and sugar. Heat gently until sugar has dissolved, then bring to the boil. Simmer for 10-15 minutes, until the cranberries have popped and softened. In a shallow dish, beat the eggs with salt and pepper. Spread breadcrumbs in another dish.

Dip cheese wedges into egg and then into breadcrumbs, making sure the cheese is completely coated. Heat oil in a deep-fat fryer to 190C (375F), or until a cube of bread browns in 40 seconds. Fry cheese portions, three at a time, for 2 minutes, until golden and crisp. Drain on kitchen paper and keep warm while frying remaining wedges. Garnish with orange rind and serve at once with cranberry relish.

Serves 6.

— BAKED AUBERGINE LAYERS —

2 large aubergines (eggplant)
1 teaspoon salt
2 red peppers (capsicum), peeled (see page 30)
70 ml (2½ fl oz/⅓ cup) olive oil
300 g (10 oz) Mozzarella cheese, thinly sliced
oregano leaves, to garnish
TOMATO SAUCE:
2 tablespoons olive oil
2 cloves garlic, crushed
700 g (1½ lb) plum tomatoes, peeled and chopped
2 teaspoons chopped fresh oregano
salt and freshly ground black pepper

Cut aubergines (eggplant) into 1 cm (½ in) thick slices. Place in a colander, sprinkle with salt and leave for 1 hour. Cut peppers (capsicum) into thin strips.

To make tomato sauce, heat olive oil in a saucepan. Add garlic and cook for a few minutes until soft. Add tomatoes, oregano and salt and pepper and cook gently, stirring, for 2 minutes, without allowing tomatoes to lose their texture. Keep warm.

Preheat oven to 180C (350F/Gas 4). Preheat grill. Rinse aubergines (eggplant) well, drain and dry thoroughly with kitchen paper. Brush with 55 ml (2 fl oz/¼ cup) of the olive oil and grill on both sides until soft and beginning to brown.

Place half the aubergine (eggplant) slices on a baking sheet. Arrange Mozzarella slices on top, cutting to fit if necessary. Top with half the pepper strips. Place remaining aubergine (eggplant) slices on top. Drizzle over remaining olive oil.

Cook in the oven for 3-5 minutes, until heated through, but do not allow Mozzarella to melt. Arrange remaining strips of pepper (capsicum) on top, garnish with oregano leaves and serve with tomato sauce.

Serves 6.

——GRILLED GOATS' CHEESE——

6 slices French bread
1 clove garlic, halved
12.5 cm (5 in) log goats' cheese
200 g (7 oz) mixed salad leaves
55 g (2 oz/ ½ cup) walnuts, roughly chopped
WALNUT DRESSING:
1 tablespoon balsamic vinegar
55 ml (2 fl oz/ ¼ cup) olive oil
2 tablespoons walnut oil
salt and freshly ground black pepper

To make walnut dressing, put vinegar, olive oil, walnut oil and salt and pepper in a bowl and whisk together. Set aside.

Preheat grill. Toast bread slices lightly on both sides. Rub one side of each slice with cut face of garlic clove. Cut goats' cheese into 6 slices and place a slice on garlic side of each slice of toast. Grill for 4-5 minutes, until slightly browned but not melting.

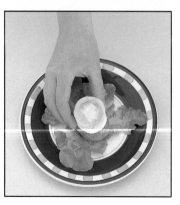

Put salad leaves in bowl, pour over dressing and toss. Arrange salad leaves on serving plates. Place goats' cheese croûtes on salad, scatter with walnuts and serve immediately.

Serves 6.

– CHICKEN & APRICOT TERRINE –

450 g (1 lb) minced chicken
225 g (8 oz) minced pork
85 g (3 oz) ready-to-eat dried apricots, coarsely
    chopped
1 clove garlic, crushed
150 ml (5 fl oz/⅔ cup) dry white wine
2 tablespoons chopped fresh mint
½ tsp ground cinnamon
salt and freshly ground black pepper
mint leaves, to garnish
APRICOT VINAIGRETTE:
25 g (1 oz) ready-to-eat dried apricots
2 teaspoons chopped fresh mint leaves
4 teaspoons white wine vinegar
70 ml (2½ fl oz/⅓ cup) olive oil

Preheat oven to 180C (350F/Gas 4). In a bowl, mix together minced chicken and minced pork. Add apricots, garlic, wine, mint, cinnamon and salt and pepper and mix well. Spoon into an 850 ml (30 fl oz/3¾ cup) terrine or loaf tin. Cover tightly with foil and put in a roasting tin. Pour boiling water into roasting tin to come halfway up sides of terrine. Bake for 1 hour, or until juices run clear. Leave to cool. Remove from tin, wrap in foil and chill overnight.

To make apricot vinaigrette, put apricots in a small saucepan and cover with water. Bring to the boil and simmer for 10-15 minutes, until soft. Drain apricots and put in a blender or food processor with mint, vinegar, oil and salt and pepper. Process until smooth. Allow terrine to come to room temperature before serving. Slice terrine, garnish with mint leaves and serve with apricot vinaigrette.

Serves 6.

PARMA HAM BASKETS

2 sheets filo pastry, 40 x 30 cm (16 x 12 in)
25 g (1 oz/2 tablespoons) butter, melted
1 tablespoon olive oil
1 red onion, finely chopped
1 teaspoon sugar
150 g (5 oz) Parma ham, coarsely chopped
10 sun-dried tomatoes, coarsely chopped
200 g (7 oz) salad leaves
basil leaves, to garnish
DRESSING:
55 ml (2 fl oz/¼ cup) olive oil
2 teaspoons wine vinegar
salt and freshly ground black pepper

Preheat oven to 190C (375F/Gas 5). Cut filo pastry into twenty-four 10 cm (4 in) squares.

Lightly brush a 12-cup bun tin with butter. Brush 12 sheets of pastry with butter. Line each cup in bun tin with a square of pastry. Brush remaining sheets of pastry with melted butter and place on top, arranging them so that the points are like petals. Bake in the oven for 10 minutes, until golden. Keep warm. Heat oil in a saucepan, add onion and cook, stirring occasionally, for 5 minutes, until soft. Add sugar and cook for 3 minutes. Stir in Parma ham and sun-dried tomatoes. Heat gently to warm through.

To make dressing, put olive oil, wine vinegar and salt and pepper in a large bowl and whisk together. Add salad leaves and toss well. Arrange salad on six serving plates. Fill tartlet cases with ham mixture. Arrange on serving plates, garnish with basil leaves and serve.

Serves 6.

PISTACHIO LIVER PÂTÉ

115 g (4 oz/½ cup) butter
2 shallots, finely chopped
2 cloves garlic, crushed
700 g (1½ lb) chicken livers, trimmed
2 tablespoons sherry
225 g (8 oz/1 cup) low-fat soft cheese
salt and freshly ground black pepper
1 teaspoon chopped fresh thyme
45 g (1½ oz/⅓ cup) pistachio nuts, coarsely chopped
thyme leaves, to garnish

Heat butter in a large frying pan, add shallots and garlic and cook for 5 minutes, stirring occasionally, until soft.

Rinse chicken livers, dry with kitchen paper and coarsely chop. Add to frying pan and cook over a moderately high heat, stirring, for 5 minutes, or until livers are browned outside and still slightly pink inside. Allow to cool slightly then put in a blender or food processor with sherry, soft cheese and salt and pepper and process until well blended. Transfer to a bowl and stir in thyme and pistachio nuts. Chill overnight.

Allow pâté to come to room temperature before serving. Shape pâté into ovals using two dessertspoons and put 2 or 3 ovals on each serving plate. Garnish with thyme leaves and serve with toasted olive bread.

Serves 6-8.

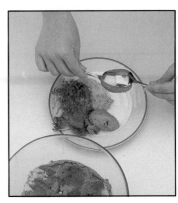

—CARIBBEAN TURKEY MOUSSE—

350 g (12 oz) minced turkey
1 small mango, peeled and roughly chopped
2 egg whites and 1 egg, beaten
grated rind and juice of 1 lime
2 cm (¾ in) piece fresh root ginger, peeled and
    grated
salt and freshly ground black pepper
115 ml (4 fl oz/ ½ cup) double (thick) cream
sunflower oil for greasing
strips of lime rind and mint leaves, to garnish
MANGO SALSA:
1 large mango, chopped
juice of 1 lime
1 fresh red chilli, cored, seeded and finely chopped
1 small red onion, finely chopped
2 tablespoons chopped fresh mint

Put minced turkey in a blender or food processor. Add mango, egg whites and egg, lime rind and juice and ginger. Process until just smooth, then season with salt and pepper. With motor running, gradually add cream until just blended. Do not over-process. Transfer mixture to a bowl, cover and chill for 30 minutes. Preheat the oven to 160C (325F/Gas 3). Lightly grease six 7.5 cm (3 in) ramekins.

Divide turkey mixture between ramekins. Smooth top and cover each one with foil. Place in a roasting tin and pour in boiling water to come halfway up the sides of ramekins. Bake for 20-25 minutes, until a skewer inserted in centre comes out clean. To make mango salsa, mix together mango, lime juice, chilli, onion, mint and salt and pepper. Chill until required. Turn mousses onto serving plates, garnish and serve hot or cold with mango salsa.

Serves 6.

CARPACCIO

450 g (1 lb) beef fillet
175 g (6 oz) rocket leaves
juice of 2 lemons
115 ml (4 fl oz/½ cup) extra virgin olive oil
freshly ground black pepper
85 g (3 oz) Parmesan cheese
capers, to garnish

Wrap beef fillet tightly in foil, seal well and freeze for 1-2 hours, until just firm but not frozen solid. Wash and dry rocket leaves and remove any thick stalks. Arrange rocket leaves on serving plates.

Unwrap steak and use a large sharp knife to cut into wafer-thin slices. Arrange beef slices, slightly overlapping, in centre of plates.

Drizzle lemon juice and olive oil over beef and season with pepper. Using a vegetable peeler, shave curls of Parmesan over beef. Garnish with capers and serve immediately.

Serves 6.

Note: A good quality olive oil is essential to the success of this dish.

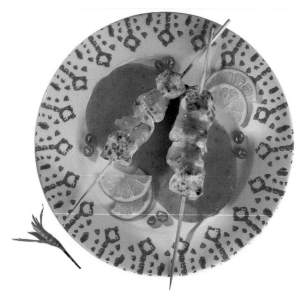

CHICKEN SATAY

juice of 1 lime
1 stalk lemon grass, finely chopped
1 clove garlic, finely chopped
2 tablespoons sunflower oil
1 teaspoon ground coriander
450 g (1 lb) boneless, skinless chicken breasts
lime slices and chilli rings, to garnish
PEANUT SAUCE:
55 g (2 oz) smooth peanut butter
150 ml (5 fl oz/⅔ cup) coconut milk
2 teaspoons Thai red curry paste
1 tablespoon Thai fish sauce
1 tablespoon soft brown sugar

Mix together lime juice, lemon grass, garlic, sunflower oil and ground coriander.

Cut chicken into 2 cm (¾ in) cubes and add to marinade. Turn to coat, cover and leave to marinate for at least 1 hour. Meanwhile, make peanut sauce. Mix together peanut butter, coconut milk, red curry paste, fish sauce and sugar and set aside. Soak twelve bamboo skewers in water for 30 minutes.

Preheat grill. Thread chicken onto skewers. Grill, turning frequently, for 8-10 minutes, until cooked through and browned on the outside. Garnish with lime slices and chilli rings and serve with peanut sauce.

Serves 6.

——PROSCIUTTO WITH FRUIT——

1 large mango
4 figs
6 physalis
6 lychees
juice of ½ lime
18 slices prosciutto
freshly ground black pepper
1 pomegranate

Peel mango and cut down either side of the narrow stone, to remove flesh. Cut away narrow band of flesh still attached to stone. Thinly slice mango flesh.

Cut figs into segments. Peel back papery skin from fruit of physalis. Peel lychees. Put all fruits in a bowl and sprinkle with lime juice.

Arrange prosciutto and fruit on serving plates. Season with pepper. Cut pomegranate in half and scoop out seeds. Scatter seeds over prosciutto and fruit and serve.

Serves 6.

Variation: Other exotic fruit may be used with prosciutto, such as melon, sharon fruit, guava, papaya or prickly pear.

—CHICKEN LIVERS & GRAPES—

450 g (1 lb) chicken livers, trimmed
salt and freshly ground black pepper
4 teaspoons olive oil
2 shallots, finely chopped
2 cloves garlic, crushed
2 tablespoons dry sherry
115 g (4 oz) seedless green grapes, halved
1 teaspoon chopped fresh rosemary
6 slices brioche
rosemary sprigs, to garnish

Rinse chicken livers and pat dry with kitchen paper. Cut into even-sized pieces. Season with salt and pepper.

Heat oil in a large frying pan. Add shallots and garlic and cook, stirring occasionally, for 5 minutes, until soft. Add chicken livers and cook over a moderately high heat, stirring, for 5 minutes, until browned on the outside and still slightly pink inside.

Add sherry, grapes and rosemary and cook, stirring, until grapes are heated through. Meanwhile, lightly toast brioche slices. Put toasted brioche on warmed serving plates and top with chicken liver mixture. Garnish with rosemary sprigs and serve immediately.

Serves 6.

TURKEY TACOS

3 tomatoes
¼ Webb's lettuce
2 tablespoons sunflower oil
1 onion, finely chopped
1 clove garlic, crushed
1 fresh green chilli, cored, seeded and finely
  chopped
115 ml (4 fl oz / ½ cup) chicken stock
225 g (8 oz) cooked turkey, shredded
1 tablespoon chopped fresh coriander
salt
6 taco shells
150 ml (5 fl oz / ⅔ cup) thick sour cream

Finely chop tomatoes and set aside. Finely shred lettuce and set aside.

Preheat oven to 180C (350F/Gas 4). Heat oil in a frying pan, add onion, garlic and chilli and cook, stirring occasionally, for 5 minutes, until soft. Add stock and boil for 5 minutes, until nearly all liquid has evaporated. Add turkey and cook for 2 minutes. Stir in coriander and salt and keep warm.

Arrange taco shells on a baking sheet and heat in the oven for 2-3 minutes. Divide shredded lettuce among ·serving plates. Spoon turkey mixture into hot shells and place on top of lettuce. Serve with diced tomato and a spoonful of soured cream.

Serves 6.

——— INDONESIAN SPARE RIBS ———

1.35 kg (3 lb) spare ribs
55 ml (2 fl oz / ¼ cup) sunflower oil
chopped spring onions and diced red pepper
　(capsicum), to garnish
MARINADE:
2.5 cm (1 in) piece fresh root ginger, peeled and
　grated
2 cloves garlic, finely chopped
1 fresh red chilli, cored, seeded and finely chopped
70 ml (2 ½ fl oz / ⅓ cup) soy sauce
juice of 1 lemon
2 tablespoons sunflower oil
2 tablespoons clear honey
1 teaspoon five-spice powder

Mix together all marinade ingredients.

Put spare ribs in a shallow, non-metallic dish, pour over marinade and turn ribs to coat thoroughly. Cover and chill for 2-3 hours, turning occasionally. Remove ribs from marinade, reserving marinade, and dry ribs with kitchen paper. Heat oil in a wok or large frying pan, add ribs and cook, in batches, for 2-3 minutes, turning, until browned.

Pour off most of oil, return ribs to pan and add marinade and enough water to cover. Bring to the boil, cover and simmer gently, stirring occasionally, for 1 hour, or until meat is tender. Boil rapidly to reduce cooking liquid to a thick sauce. Arrange ribs and sauce on warmed serving plates. Garnish with chopped spring onions and diced red pepper (capsicum) and serve.

Serves 6.

SAFFRON MUSSELS

3 kg (6 lb) mussels
3 tablespoons dry cider
SAFFRON SAUCE:
2 tablespoons olive oil
3 shallots, finely chopped
1 clove garlic, crushed
175 ml (6 fl oz/¾ cup) dry cider
large pinch of saffron strands
freshly ground black pepper
25 g (1 oz/2 tablespoons) butter
2 tablespoons chopped fresh parsley

Discard broken mussels and any which do not close when tapped sharply. Scrape off any barnacles, remove 'beards' and scrub.

To make saffron sauce, heat olive oil in a saucepan. Add shallots and garlic and cook, stirring occasionally, for 5 minutes, until soft. Set aside. Put mussels and cider in a large saucepan. Bring to the boil, cover tightly and cook over a high heat, shaking pan occasionally, for 4-5 minutes, until mussels have opened.

Remove mussels with a slotted spoon, discarding any that have not opened. Transfer to warmed serving plates and keep warm. Line a sieve with muslin, place over a measuring jug and strain cooking liquid. Add 150 ml (5 fl oz/⅔ cup) cooking liquid to shallots and garlic. Add cider, saffron and pepper. Bring to the boil and boil until reduced by one-third. Whisk in butter. Stir in parsley, pour over mussels and serve.

Serves 6.

—MEDITERRANEAN SCALLOPS—

700 g (1 ½ lb) shelled scallops
3 tablespoons olive oil
1 clove garlic, crushed
4 teaspoons fresh thyme leaves
salt and freshly ground black pepper
MEDITERRANEAN VEGETABLES:
2 tablespoons olive oil
1 shallot, finely chopped
1 clove garlic, crushed
1 aubergine (eggplant), diced
2 courgettes (zucchini), diced
1 red and 1 yellow pepper (capsicum), diced
juice of ½ lemon
1 tablespoon chopped fresh oregano

Rinse scallops, dry with kitchen paper and cut in half. Place in a bowl with oil, garlic, thyme and salt and pepper. Mix well, cover and chill. To prepare Mediterranean vegetables, heat oil in a frying pan, add shallot and garlic and cook, stirring occasionally, for 5 minutes, until soft. Add aubergine (eggplant), courgettes (zucchini) and peppers (capsicum) and stir-fry over a high heat until softened but still retaining some texture. Keep warm.

Heat a large heavy frying pan. Add scallops in one layer and cook for 1 minute. Turn and cook other side for 1 minute. Add lemon juice, oregano and salt and pepper to vegetables. Arrange vegetables in scallop shells or on serving plates, place scallops on top and serve.

Serves 6.

Note: If the scallops have their coral with them you can use that too.

—PRAWN & LETTUCE PARCELS—

2 crisp lettuces
1 tablespoon olive oil
1 bunch of spring onions, chopped
1 clove garlic, crushed
1 red pepper (capsicum), diced
225 g (8 oz) large cooked, peeled prawns
4 teaspoons chopped fresh chives
salt and freshly ground black pepper
300 ml (10 fl oz/1¼ cups) dry white wine
300 ml (10 fl oz/1¼ cups) fish stock
115 g (4 oz/½ cup) butter, diced
1 teaspoon pink peppercorns
chives and red pepper (capsicum) strips, to garnish

Separate 12 large leaves from lettuces and wash thoroughly. Bring a large pan of water to the boil, add lettuce leaves and blanch for 30 seconds. Drain and plunge into a bowl of cold water. Spread on a tea towel and leave to drain. Heat oil in a saucepan, add spring onions, garlic and red pepper (capsicum) and cook, stirring occasionally, for 3 minutes. Add prawns, half chives and salt and pepper.

Divide filling among lettuce leaves and wrap up to form parcels. Put wine and stock in a saucepan. Bring to the boil and boil rapidly until reduced by half. Add parcels and heat gently to warm through. Remove with a slotted spoon, transfer to warmed serving plates and keep warm. Whisk butter into sauce, a little at a time, until thickened. Stir in remaining chives and pink peppercorns. Pour around parcels, garnish with chives and red pepper (capsicum) strips and serve.

Serves 6.

THAI SQUID SALAD

800 g (1¾ lb) fresh squid
juice of 1 lime
2 tablespoons Thai fish sauce
1 fresh red chilli, cored, seeded and finely chopped
1 clove garlic, crushed
2.5 cm (1 in) piece fresh root ginger, peeled and
    grated
2 stalks lemon grass, thinly sliced
6 spring onions, thinly sliced
2 tablespoons chopped fresh coriander
10 mint leaves, coarsely chopped
200 g (7 oz) salad leaves
chilli rings, to garnish

To clean squid, pull head and tentacles away from body sac and discard.

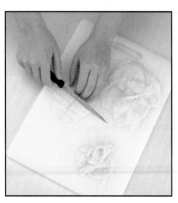

Remove innards and discard. Remove transparent 'quill' from body. Remove any purple skin from body. Rinse body sac thoroughly and slit open. Score the inside of body sac in a criss-cross pattern, then cut into 1 x 5 cm (½ x 2 in) strips. Bring a saucepan of water to the boil.

Add squid and simmer for 1 minute, until opaque. Drain and put into a bowl. Add lime juice, fish sauce, chilli, garlic, ginger, lemon grass and spring onions. Cover and leave to marinate for at least 1 hour. Stir in coriander and mint. Arrange salad leaves on serving plates, top with squid mixture, garnish with chilli rings and serve.

Serves 6.

SALMON MOUSSE

sunflower oil for greasing
350 g (12 oz) skinless salmon fillet
115 g (4 oz/½ cup) curd cheese
115 ml (4 fl oz/½ cup) plain yogurt
2 eggs, beaten
salt and freshly ground black pepper
2 teaspoons lemon juice
1 tablespoon chopped fresh dill
dill sprigs, to garnish
SORREL SAUCE:
1 tablespoon butter
115 g (4 oz) sorrel, washed, dried and very finely
  chopped
150 ml (5 fl oz/⅔ cup) whipping cream

Preheat oven to 160C (325F/Gas 3). Lightly oil six 115 ml (4 fl oz/½ cup) moulds. Cut salmon into cubes and put in a blender or food processor with curd cheese, yogurt, eggs and salt and pepper. Process until smooth. Add lemon juice and dill and process briefly. Spoon mixture into prepared moulds then place in a roasting tin. Pour in boiling water to come one-third of the way up sides of moulds. Cover each one with foil and bake for about 20 minutes, until a skewer inserted in centre comes out clean.

Meanwhile, make sorrel sauce. Heat butter in a saucepan, add sorrel and cook, stirring, for 2-3 minutes, until softened. Stir in cream and salt and pepper, bring to the boil and simmer for 2-3 minutes, to thicken slightly. Turn each mousse onto a warmed serving plate, pour a little sorrel sauce around the mousse, garnish with dill sprigs and serve.

Serves 6.

SEAFOOD DIAMONDS

350 g (12 oz) puff pastry, thawed if frozen
1 egg, beaten
225 g (8 oz) smoked haddock fillet
225 g (8 oz) monkfish fillet
225 g (8 oz) leeks
25 g (1 oz/2 tablespoons) butter
2 teaspoons plain flour
150 ml (5 fl oz/⅔ cup) dry white wine
large pinch of saffron strands
2 teaspoons lemon juice
salt and freshly ground black pepper
55 ml (2 fl oz/¼ cup) double (thick) cream
115 g (4 oz) cooked, peeled prawns
salad leaves, to garnish

Preheat oven to 220C (425F/Gas 7). Roll out pastry on a lightly floured surface until 3 mm (⅛ in) thick. Cut out twelve diamonds and arrange on a baking sheet. Brush pastry with beaten egg. Bake in the oven for 10 minutes, until well risen and golden brown. Split each diamond in half horizontally and keep warm.

Put smoked haddock in a saucepan, cover with cold water, bring to the boil and simmer for 5 minutes, until just cooked. Remove haddock, reserving cooking liquid. Flake fish into a bowl, discarding skin. Cut monkfish into 2 cm (¾ in) cubes. Add monkfish to cooking liquid and cook for 5 minutes. Remove with a slotted spoon, reserving cooking liquid, and add monkfish to bowl.

Cut leeks lengthways in half and thinly slice.
Heat butter in a saucepan, add leeks and
cook, stirring occasionally, for 5-10 minutes,
until soft. Stir in flour and cook, stirring, for
1 minute. Stir in 150 ml (5 fl oz/⅔ cup)
reserved fish cooking liquid, bring to the boil
and simmer for 2 minutes.

Put wine and saffron in a small saucepan,
bring to the boil and boil rapidly until
reduced to 2 tablespoons. Strain into leek
sauce. Stir in lemon juice and salt and
pepper. Add cream, haddock, monkfish and
prawns and heat gently to warm through.

Arrange bottom halves of two pastry
diamonds on each warmed serving plate.
Spoon over fish mixture and top with glazed
pastry lids. Garnish and serve.

Serves 6.

PRAWN & FETA PURSES

115 g (4 oz) cooked, peeled prawns
225 g (8 oz) feta cheese
1 clove garlic, crushed
2 tablespoons chopped fresh dill
grated rind of 1 lime
salt and freshly ground black pepper
3 sheets filo pastry, 40 x 30 cm (16 x 12 in)
25 g (1 oz/2 tablespoons) butter, melted
dill sprigs and lime wedges, to garnish
DILL SAUCE:
150 ml (5 fl oz/⅔ cup) thick sour cream
150 ml (5 fl oz/⅔ cup) whipping cream, whipped
1 teaspoon lime juice
2 teaspoons chopped fresh dill

Preheat oven to 200C (400F/Gas 6). Coarsely
chop prawns and put in a bowl. Crumble in
feta cheese, then add garlic, dill, lime rind
and salt and pepper. Cut each sheet of filo
pastry into 12 squares. Lightly brush each
square with melted butter. Lay two squares
on top of one another, arranging points at an
angle like petals. Put a teaspoon of prawn
filling in centre and pull up pastry, pinching
together above filling to make a purse.
Repeat to make 18 purses.

Brush a baking sheet with melted butter.
Place purses on baking sheet, brush with a
little melted butter and bake in the oven for
10-15 minutes, until golden. Meanwhile,
make dill sauce. In a bowl, mix together thick
sour cream, whipping cream, lime juice, dill
and salt and pepper. Garnish purses with dill
sprigs and lime wedges and serve with sauce.

Serves 6.

SMOKED TROUT MOUSSE

575 g (1 ¼ lb) thinly sliced smoked trout
150 g (5 oz/⅔ cup) cream cheese
150 ml (5 fl oz/⅔ cup) Greek yogurt
juice of ½ lemon
salt and freshly ground black pepper
pinch of cayenne pepper
tarragon sprigs, to garnish
CUCUMBER VINAIGRETTE:
70 ml (2 ½ fl oz/⅓ cup) light olive oil
juice of ½ lemon
1 tablespoon chopped fresh tarragon
⅛ cucumber, seeded and finely diced

Line six 115 ml (4 fl oz/½ cup) ramekins with
cling film. Line with half the smoked trout.

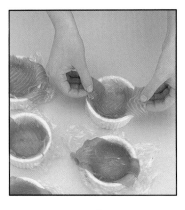

Put remaining smoked trout in a blender or
food processor with cream cheese, yogurt,
lemon juice, salt and cayenne pepper. Process
until smooth. Spoon into lined ramekins,
fold overhanging trout and cling film over
the top and chill for at least 4 hours.

To make the cucumber vinaigrette, whisk
together oil and lemon juice. Stir in tarragon,
cucumber and salt and pepper. Turn each
mousse out onto a serving plate and remove
cling film. Garnish with tarragon sprigs and
serve with cucumber vinaigrette.

Serves 6.

—FISH & WATERCRESS TERRINE—

¼ cucumber, very thinly sliced
450 g (1 lb) sole fillets
70 ml (2½ fl oz/⅓ cup) dry white wine
1 tablespoon lemon juice
2 bay leaves
4 black peppercorns
1 tablespoon powdered gelatine
225 g (8 oz/1 cup) cream cheese
115 g (4 oz) watercress, stalks removed
115 ml (4 fl oz/½ cup) double (thick) cream
salt and freshly ground black pepper
115 g (4 oz) thinly sliced smoked salmon
lemon slices, lemon rind and sprigs of watercress, to
    garnish
WATERCRESS SAUCE:
25 g (1 oz) watercress, stalks removed
250 ml (9 fl oz/1 cup) crème fraîche
1 tablespoon lemon juice

Spread cucumber slices on kitchen paper,
sprinkle with salt and leave to drain. Line a
1 litre (35 fl oz/4½ cup) terrine or loaf tin
with cling film. Place sole in a saucepan. Add
wine, 70 ml (2½ fl oz/⅓ cup) water, lemon
juice, bay leaves and peppercorns. Bring
slowly to the boil, cover and simmer gently
for 10 minutes, until fish flakes easily.
Remove fish, reserving cooking liquid and
flake fish, discarding skin.

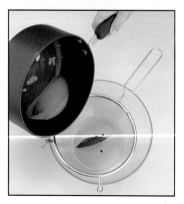

Put 70 ml (2½ fl oz/⅓ cup) warm water in a
large bowl, sprinkle over gelatine and leave
for 5 minutes, until absorbed. Bring fish
cooking liquid to the boil and boil rapidly
until reduced by half. Strain into bowl of
gelatine and stir until gelatine has dissolved.

Put sole in a blender or food processor with cream cheese and process until blended. With motor running, pour gelatine mixture onto fish mixture and blend. Remove three-quarters of mixture, transfer to a bowl and set aside. Add watercress to blender and process briefly. Transfer to a bowl. Lightly whip cream. Fold just under half of cream into watercress mixture and remainder into white fish mixture.

Season both mixtures with salt and pepper. Dry cucumber with kitchen paper and arrange half in base of terrine. Spread half white fish mixture over base of tin and cover with half smoked salmon. Cover with watercress mixture and then the remaining smoked salmon. Top with remaining white fish mixture. Cover with remaining cucumber. Cover tin and chill for 4 hours.

To make watercress sauce, put watercress, crème fraîche, lemon juice and salt and pepper in a blender or food processor and process until smooth. Turn out terrine and slice. Garnish and serve with watercress sauce.

Serves 6-8.

—MUSSEL & FENNEL TARTLETS—

1 quantity shortcrust pastry (see page 82)
1.35 kg (3 lb) mussels, trimmed (see page 99)
115 ml (4 fl oz/ ½ cup) dry white wine
25 g (1 oz/2 tablespoons) butter
1 bunch of spring onions, finely chopped
1 clove garlic, crushed
1 large fennel bulb, halved and thinly sliced
2 teaspoons lemon juice
55 ml (2 fl oz/ ¼ cup) double (thick) cream
salt and freshly ground black pepper
fennel leaves, to garnish

Preheat oven to 200C (400F/Gas 6). Roll out pastry on a lightly floured surface and use to line six 10 cm (4 in) loose-bottomed tartlet tins. Line with foil or greaseproof paper.

Fill with baking beans and bake in the oven for 10 minutes. Remove foil and beans and bake for 2-3 minutes, until pastry is cooked and golden. Keep warm. Put mussels in a large saucepan with 2 tablespoons white wine. Bring to the boil, cover tightly and cook over a high heat, shaking pan occasionally, for 4-5 minutes, until mussels open. Drain, reserving cooking liquid and discarding any mussels that have not opened. Remove mussels from shells, discarding shells, and keep warm.

Heat butter in a saucepan. Add spring onions, garlic and fennel and cook, stirring occasionally, for 5 minutes, until soft. Add remaining white wine, lemon juice and 70 ml (2 ½ fl oz/⅓ cup) reserved mussel cooking liquid. Simmer until reduced by half. Add cream and boil for a few minutes until thickened. Season with salt and pepper. Add mussels to fennel mixture and heat gently to warm through. Spoon into pastry cases. Garnish with fennel and serve.

Serves 6.

MONKFISH TEMPURA

450 g (1 lb) monkfish fillets
sunflower oil for deep-frying
BATTER:
115 g (4 oz/1 cup) plain flour
1 egg, beaten
1 egg yolk
RED PEPPER (CAPSICUM) SALSA:
½ red onion, finely diced
1 fresh green chilli, cored, seeded and chopped
1 red pepper (capsicum), finely diced
2 tablespoons lemon juice
1 tablespoon chopped fresh parsley
salt

Mix together all ingredients for red pepper (capsicum) salsa. Cover and chill until required.

Cut monkfish into strips. To make batter, sift flour into a bowl and whisk in egg, egg yolk and 175 ml (6 fl oz/¾ cup) iced water. Heat 5 cm (2 in) sunflower oil in a large, deep frying pan or wok.

Dip monkfish strips into batter and fry, in batches, until crisp and pale golden. Drain on kitchen paper and keep warm while cooking remainder. Divide among serving plates and serve with red pepper (capsicum) salsa.

Serves 6.

THAI CRAB CAKES

25 g (1 oz/2 tablespoons) butter
25 g (1 oz/¼ cup) plain flour
150 ml (5 fl oz/⅔ cup) milk
350 g (12 oz) dressed crab
2 teaspoons chopped fresh coriander
150 g (5 oz/2½ cups) fresh breadcrumbs
grated rind of ½ lime
2 teaspoons lime juice
4 spring onions, finely chopped
1 teaspoon Thai green curry paste
2 teaspoons Thai fish sauce
1 egg, beaten
70 ml (2½ fl oz/⅓ cup) sunflower oil
lime slices and coriander leaves, to garnish

Heat butter in a saucepan. Add flour and cook, stirring, for 1 minute. Remove from heat and gradually stir in milk. Simmer, stirring, for 2-3 minutes, until thickened. Remove from heat. Stir in crab, coriander, 25 g (1 oz/½ cup) breadcrumbs, lime rind and juice, spring onions, curry paste and fish sauce. Leave to cool. Spread mixture into a round and cut into 12 wedges. With floured hands, shape each wedge into a round cake.

Put remaining breadcrumbs on a plate and put beaten egg in a shallow dish. Dip each crab cake in beaten egg and then in breadcrumbs, to coat thoroughly. Chill for 15 minutes. Heat oil in a frying pan and fry crab cakes for 3-4 minutes on each side, until crisp and golden. Garnish with lime slices and coriander leaves and serve.

Serves 6.

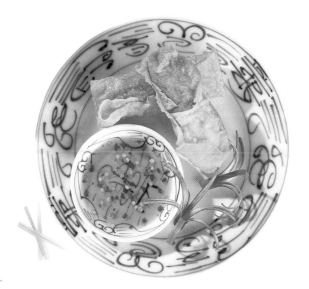

──CHICKEN & CRAB ROLLS──

12 spring roll wrappers
225 g (8 oz) cooked chicken, finely chopped
115 g (4 oz) dressed crab
4 spring onions, finely chopped
1 small carrot, grated
2 teaspoons Thai fish sauce
2 teaspoons soy sauce
1 clove garlic, crushed
2 small sticks celery, finely diced
12 small, crisp lettuce leaves
sunflower oil for deep-frying
spring onion tassels, to garnish
chilli dipping sauce, to serve

Place spring roll wrappers between two damp tea towels, to soften.

In a bowl, mix together chicken, crab, spring onions, carrot, fish sauce, soy sauce, garlic and celery. Place a lettuce leaf in middle of each spring roll wrapper. Place a spoonful of chicken mixture on each lettuce leaf. Fold over three sides of wrapper to enclose filling. Roll up firmly.

Heat oil in a wok or deep-fat fryer to 190C (375F), or until a cube of bread will brown in 40 seconds. Add rolls and fry, in batches, for 3 minutes, or until crisp and golden. Drain on kitchen paper. Garnish with spring onion tassels and serve with chilli dipping sauce.

Serves 6.

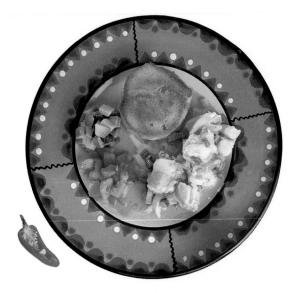

MEXICAN SEVICHE

450 g (1 lb) skinless cod fillets
1 bunch of spring onions, thinly sliced
juice of 1 orange and 5 limes
3 tablespoons olive oil
1 fresh green chilli, cored, seeded and chopped
salt
1 avocado
2 tomatoes
CORNMEAL PANCAKES:
55 g (2 oz/ ½ cup) self-raising flour
55 g (2 oz/ ⅓ cup) polenta
1 teaspoon baking powder
½ fresh red chilli, cored, seeded and chopped
1 egg, beaten
115 ml (4 fl oz/ ½ cup) milk
sunflower oil for frying

Cut fish into bite-sized pieces and put in a non-metallic dish with spring onions and orange and lime juice. Mix well, cover and chill for 3 hours, until fish becomes opaque and looks cooked. Stir in olive oil, chilli and ½ teaspoon salt, cover and chill for 1 hour. To make cornmeal pancakes, put flour, polenta, baking powder, ½ teaspoon salt and chilli into a bowl. Mix together egg and milk, add to dry ingredients and mix to form a smooth batter.

Heat a little oil in a frying pan. Drop spoonfuls of batter onto pan to make 6 small pancakes and cook for 2-3 minutes on each side, until cooked through and golden brown. Remove and keep warm. Halve avocado lengthways, remove stone and peel. Dice avocado flesh and tomatoes. Serve seviche with cornmeal pancakes, avocado and tomatoes.

Serves 6.

—CRAB WITH TOMATO SALSA—

12-18 crab claws
TOMATO SALSA:
450 g (1 lb) tomatoes, peeled
½ small red onion, finely chopped
3 spring onions, finely chopped
1 fresh green chilli, cored, seeded and finely
   chopped
2 tablespoons chopped fresh coriander
2 teaspoons lemon juice
salt and freshly ground black pepper
CORN CHIPS:
6 corn tortillas
olive oil for brushing

Preheat oven to 200C (400F/Gas 6). To make tomato salsa, chop tomatoes into tiny dice.

Mix together tomato, red onion, spring onions, chilli, coriander, lemon juice and salt and pepper. Chill until required.

To make corn chips, brush tortillas with oil and cut into quarters. Arrange in a single layer on a baking sheet. Bake in the oven for 10 minutes, until golden and crisp. Serve crab claws with tomato salsa and corn chips.

Serves 6.

—GRILLED STUFFED MUSSELS—

2.75 kg (6 lb) mussels, trimmed (see page 99)
55 ml (2 fl oz/¼ cup) dry white wine
115 g (4 oz/½ cup) butter, softened
1 clove garlic, crushed
2 shallots, very finely chopped
55 ml (2 fl oz/¼ cup) pesto
salt and freshly ground black pepper
25 g (1 oz/½ cup) fresh breadcrumbs
25 g (1 oz/¼ cup) grated Parmesan cheese
basil leaves, to garnish

Put mussels and wine in a large saucepan. Bring to the boil, cover tightly and cook over a high heat, shaking the pan occasionally, for 4-5 minutes, until mussels open.

Line a grill pan with crumpled foil. Drain mussels, discarding any that remain closed. Remove top shell from each mussel and arrange lower shells on grill pan. In a bowl, mix together butter, garlic, shallots, pesto and salt and pepper.

Preheat grill. Spoon a little butter mixture onto each mussel. In a bowl, mix together breadcrumbs and Parmesan cheese and sprinkle over mussels. Grill for 5 minutes, until bubbling and golden. Garnish with basil leaves and serve immediately.

Serves 6.

Variation: This dish can also be made with clams.

SEARED TUNA

575 g (1 ¼ lb) piece tuna loin
1 tablespoon soy sauce
2 tablespoons mixed peppercorns, crushed
sunflower oil for greasing
TOMATO & ANCHOVY SALSA:
4 tomatoes, seeded and diced
50 g (2 oz) can anchovies in olive oil
1 clove garlic, crushed
2 tablespoons olive oil
2 tablespoons chopped fresh parsley
salt and freshly ground black pepper

Brush tuna with soy sauce. Press crushed peppercorns all over fish.

Heat a heavy frying pan or ridged grill pan until very hot, then brush with oil. Add tuna and cook over a high heat for 2 minutes per side. Leave to cool then chill until required.

To make tomato and anchovy salsa, put tomatoes in a bowl. Drain anchovies and coarsely chop. Add to tomatoes with garlic, olive oil, parsley and salt and pepper and mix well. Using a long sharp knife, thinly slice tuna. Arrange tuna slices on serving plates with tomato and anchovy salsa and serve.

Serves 6.

SPICY KING PRAWNS

2 cloves garlic, crushed
1 small bunch of coriander, finely chopped
juice of 2 limes
1 fresh red chilli, cored, seeded and finely chopped
70 ml (2½ fl oz/⅓ cup) sunflower oil
24 large raw prawns
GUACAMOLE:
1 clove garlic, crushed
4 tomatoes, peeled and finely chopped
1 fresh green chilli, cored, seeded and finely
   chopped
juice of 1 lime
2 tablespoons chopped fresh coriander
salt and freshly ground black pepper
1 large ripe avocado

In a shallow non-metallic dish, mix together garlic, coriander, lime juice, chilli and sunflower oil. Add prawns and mix well. Cover and chill for 1-2 hours, turning occasionally. To make guacamole, put garlic, tomatoes, chilli, lime juice, coriander and salt and pepper in a bowl and mix well. Halve avocado lengthways and remove stone. Using a teaspoon, scoop out flesh, taking care to scrape away dark green flesh closest to skin. Mash into tomato mixture. Preheat grill.

Remove prawns from marinade and arrange on grill rack. Grill for 2-3 minutes on each side, basting with marinade. Serve with guacamole and tortilla chips.

Serves 6.

Note: Don't prepare the guacamole more than 30 minutes in advance or the avocado will discolour.

─────OYSTERS MEXICANA─────

24 oysters
2 tomatoes, peeled and finely diced
4 spring onions, finely chopped
1 fresh red chilli, cored, seeded and finely chopped
2 tablespoons chopped fresh parsley
juice of 1 lemon
seaweed, to garnish

Place oysters on top of cracked ice, to keep chilled. Wrap a tea towel around one hand. Hold oyster, flat side up and insert blade of an oyster knife, or a short, rigid knife, into hinge of oyster shell. Push and twist knife to prise open the shell. Discard top shell.

Slide knife under oyster to detach it from lower shell, taking care not to lose any juice. Embed each oyster in ice until ready to serve.

In a bowl, mix together tomatoes, spring onions, chilli and parsley. Spread cracked ice on serving plates and arrange oysters on top. Spoon a little of the tomato mixture over each oyster, then sprinkle over a little lemon juice. Garnish with seaweed and serve.

Serves 4.

INDEX